52 weeks of tranquility journal

by Kimberly Wilson

Sending love, Kimberly

Copyright 2015 by Kimberly Wilson

All rights reserved. This book may not be reproduced in whole or in part, stored in a retrieval system, or transmitted in any form or by any means—electronic, mechanical, or other—without written permission from the publisher, except by a reviewer, who may quote brief passages in a review.

Tranquilista, Tranquilologie, Tranquil Space, Hip Tranquil Chick, TranquiliT, and Tranquil Space Foundation are registered trademarks.

DISCLAIMER: This publication contains the opinions and ideas of its author. The advice contained herein is for informational purposes only. Please consult a medical professional before beginning any diet or exercise program. The author disclaims all responsibility for any liability, loss, risk, injury, or damage resulting from the use, proper or improper, of any of the contents contained in this book. Every effort has been made to ensure that the information contained in this book is complete and accurate.

First printing, December 2015
ISBN: 978-1522727330
Printed in the United States of America

iPhoneography by Kimberly Wilson
Text design and typography by Christy Jenkins • holeyheart.com

Acknowledgements

Many special beings helped make this project possible, including:

Tim Mooney, who is my best friend, cheerleader, and right hand.

Mama, Linda Wilson, who regularly and gleefully proclaims that I'm her favorite daughter in the whole wide world and caught various typos along the way. (Author's note: I'm her only daughter).

Pops, Steve Wilson, who inspired the writing craft and love of photography at an early age.

Mookie Wilson Mooney, who helped heal a broken heart.

Teams at Tranquil Space, TranquiliT, and Tranquil Space Foundation, who keep me inspired with their passion for spreading tranquility.

Designer Christy Jenkins, who beautifully brings my vision to life.

Writing teacher Heather Sellers, who graciously shares her gift of the written word.

Beta readers Catherine Pickard, Alison Day, Darca Tkach, Pam Barnes, Sonja Barisic, Ginger Wiseman, Katherine Dimas, Regina Hughes, and Jessica Goody, who generously offered their editing eyes to this project.

Table of Contents

Introduction 7
Testimonials 8
52 Weeks Checklist 10
50 Things to Experience 12
24 Books to Read 13
10 Places to Visit 13
Start + Stop List 14
Gratitude List 15
Inspiration Spread 16

Week 1-52
- Week 1: Let It Percolate 18
- Week 2: Choose Your Theme 20
- Week 3: Meditate 22
- Week 4: Clear Clutter 24
- Week 5: Sun Salute 26
- Week 6: Single-Task 28
- Week 7: Be Present 30
- Week 8: Artist's Date 32
- Week 9: Snail Mail 34
- Week 10: Try Something New 36
- Week 11: Seasonal Reflection 38
- Week 12: Your Insides, Another's Outsides 40
- Week 13: Take a Break 42
- Week 14: Get Outside 44
- Week 15: Capture the Moment 46
- Week 16: Let Go 48
- Week 17: A.M. Routine 50
- Week 18: Add Beauty 52
- Week 19: Get Away 54
- Week 20: Read 56
- Week 21: Carve Your Path 58
- Week 22: Breathe 60
- Week 23: *Fleurs* 62
- Week 24: Sip Tea 64
- Week 25: Eat Your Veggies 66
- Week 26: Write 68
- Week 27: Pen Month's Dreams 70
- Week 28: P.M. Routine 72
- Week 29: Mindful Eating 74
- Week 30: Practice Acceptance 76
- Week 31: Embrace Minimalism 78
- Week 32: Drink Your Greens 80
- Week 33: Walk 82
- Week 34: Signature Style 84
- Week 35: Journal 86
- Week 36: Oil Up 88
- Week 37: Soak in the Tub 90
- Week 38: Entertain 92
- Week 39: Review Budget 94
- Week 40: Volunteer 96
- Week 41: Create 98
- Week 42: Productivity 100
- Week 43: Body Scan 102
- Week 44: Self-Care 104
- Week 45: Disconnect 106
- Week 46: Bed Day 108
- Week 47: Gratitude 110
- Week 48: Move Mindfully 112
- Week 49: Practice Yin 114
- Week 50: Hollydaze 116
- Week 51: Be Kind 118
- Week 52: Reflect 120

5 Bonus Weeks
- Bonus 1: Beauty Routine 122
- Bonus 2: De-stress 124
- Bonus 3: Capsule Wardrobe 126
- Bonsu 4: Hydrate 128
- Bonus 5: Accessorize 130

Savvy Sources 132
Farewell 134
About the Author 135

This *Journal* is dedicated to the readers around the globe who participated in the *52 Weeks of Tranquility* program.

Introduction

The New Year. A fresh beginning. Ever notice how it starts strong with promises and good intentions, yet by mid-January that enthusiasm fades? Me, too!

So one chilly December evening I sat fireside with a steaming cuppa tea, snoring pug, and my laptop to pen a blog post promising to create a program to help us stay motivated and engaged throughout the year.

A jovial holiday spirit and a desire to remain mindful of good intentions are responsible for the output of 24,000 words, over 250 hours of writing, and weekly passion poured into the 52 Weeks of Tranquility program.

Throughout 2015, hundreds joined the 52 Weeks of Tranquility Facebook group from far and wide to connect, share stories and photos, ask questions, and explore weekly nuggets on living with more tranquility.

This 52 Weeks of Tranquility Journal takes you through a full year with ongoing encouragement to dig deep, slow down, and reflect. Start with Week 1 or choose what speaks to you from the Table of Contents and dive in.

A complementary photograph from Parisian travels or everyday escapades and a blank page accompany each of the inspiring essays. Capture your experience around the week's idea on the journal page. Note what speaks to you, jot down what you practiced, and explore how it felt. Highlight what you'll take away from that week.

Essays such as "Let Go," "Move Mindfully," "Try Something New," "Drink Your Greens," "Single Task," and "Capture the Moment" offer readers new ideas and reinforce familiar ones.

In addition, you'll find a few bonus essays, Savvy Sources, and a link to online resources to help fill your next 52 weeks with mindfulness, simplicity, elegance, and tranquility.

My wish is to offer a gentle nudge out of your comfort zone while also encouraging self-acceptance and meaning-making this year and beyond.

kimberlywilson.com/52weeks

Testimonials

This year, I followed Kimberly's *52 Weeks of Tranquility*. Each week I eagerly awaited the new post, and if I was busy, I saved it. I wanted to allow time to read and reflect on what she had to say, suggest, or offer as inspiration. Time and time again, I was amazed to find that the weekly topic aligned with something going on in my own life. How in the world did she know I needed to think about being present? Or that it was time to take a look at the food I eat? Who told Kimberly that I needed help creating a morning/evening routine? Gracious, does everyone know that I need to up my greens and work on my style?

~ Helen Landi

Week by week, my superpowers were revealed. I found the power to "make someone's day" by writing an old fashioned letter – an unexpected treasure in a mailbox usually filled with junk mail and bills. I discovered the power of meditation and single tasking. By being present, I began to notice and find things I might have been too distracted to see before.

I've always written checks for charity, but this year I walked 1200 miles for water, mosquito nets, the homeless, animals and veterans. If you could see the x-rays of my battered knees, you'd know how astonishing this is.

52 Weeks of Tranquility helped me uncover my creative side (as a computer programmer, I didn't even know I had one – huh) infusing more joy and fun, as well as more meaning and kindness into my days. No beating yourself up for what you didn't get done. Instead, look at how you made a difference – progress not perfection.

~ Jo Cruz

I have really enjoyed receiving the *52 Weeks of Tranquility* each week in my inbox. Each short essay is jam packed with great suggestions, information and pointers. Just reading the ideas Kimberly offers have kept me grounded through a year of many changes. They have helped me strengthen my foundation while adding some lightness. It's a wonderful combination! Can't wait for the hard copy!

~ Catherine Pickard

Days merge into weeks, weeks into months and before you can reflect on your new year goals, twelve months have passed. The treadmill of living offers no pause for reflection, unless prodded to do so…. and that is precisely what the *52 Weeks of Tranquility* does. Weekly emails have enabled the pushing of the mythical pause button every 7 days, enabling focused reflection, the setting of future intentions and the opportunity to write action points (in a list-got to love a list!) which can be applied to the day-to-day in small, manageable chunks.

Themes such as 'signature style', 'getting outside' and 'drinking your veggies' appeared in my inbox, perfectly capturing the changing seasons. For that designated week, the chosen theme was my focus. Small tweaks were made to my routine…. wearing a bracelet that I had never worn before, or ensuring that I bundled up and headed out to the park with the family on a bitter winters day. Each gentle e-mail nudge from Kimberly created a response, which cumulatively resulted in significant change after 52 weeks. Progress is not linear and some weeks, new habits developed which were later forgotten, only to be rediscovered in a later season. However, on reflection, positive patterns were born, which will be carried over and built on in future years.

~ Alison Day

I have greatly benefited from *52 Weeks of Tranquility*. It came into my life during a time of, let's say, an identity crisis. As a full-time homemaker/mother, whose son is now an adult about to leave the nest, I needed to start finding my way back to me. Mildly depressed with too much empty time on my hands, I began to seek out the next chapter of my life. *52 Weeks of Tranquility* offered a pathway to both nurturing myself (for a change), and finding myself. The inspiration and comfort I've gained from this program is immeasurable. Thank you so much for sharing it. Also, as a fellow animal lover and vegetarian, I adore your commitment to animals. That made it even easier for me to open up and let your words soak in. Kindred spirits, I'd say.

~ Teri Liptak

This year was a year I desperately needed tranquility. It was a year filled with transition and change. Having *52 Weeks of Tranquility* pop into my inbox every week served as a landmark of comfort in a year of the wild, unchartered unknown. *52 Weeks of Tranquility* helped remind me that I didn't have to kick and scream my way through the unfamiliar terrain I found myself in. Instead, I remembered each week through Kimberly's writing that while I found myself in an unknown juncture of life, it was up to me how I navigated things. So, with *52 Weeks of Tranquility* serving as one of my roadmaps of the heart, I embarked on the journey of finding peace in the adventure of my life.

It's so easy in today's world to forget to take care of the one person we need to take care of first: ourselves. Kimberly's reminders to take care of myself by choosing to breathe fully, soak in steaming baths, select nourishing foods, bookend my days through an A.M. and P.M. routine, and mindfully experience my moments breathed life into the stale corners of my being. I'm so grateful for the *52 Weeks of Tranquility*!

~ Kylie Grethen Howell

The Facebook Group and weekly email were so helpful for connecting to others of a like mind as well as sharing insightful and fun links, mindful practices, and tranquil prompts with us and for what others are doing with their planners and their *52 Weeks of Tranquility*.

When things in my life started going off course willy nilly, Kimberly's *52 Weeks of Tranquility* was a gentle reminder that even when things go wonky it is okay for me to come out of my head space and focus on being fully present in the moment, using my breath, a yoga posture, and practicing mindfulness.

~ Eva Wright

I have been following Kimberly's offerings for the past 8 years and have found such inspiration in her work. *52 Weeks of Tranquility* has been such an important reminder for me on slowing down and appreciating life. I enjoyed reading Kimberly's essays each week and developed a toolbox on ideas for living in tranquility. I love the variety of ideas presented and I think this journal project is the PERFECT reflection piece that can really help me to instill these practices on a regular basis.

~ Rachal Edwards

I have really enjoyed receiving *52 Weeks of Tranquility* each week in my inbox. Each short essay is jam packed with great suggestions, information and pointers. Just reading the ideas Kimberly offers have kept me grounded through a year of many changes. They have helped me strengthen my foundation while adding some lightness. It's a wonderful combination! Can't wait for the hard copy!

~ Catherine Pickard

Your writing has inspired me to stop feeling negative about what I didn't do, focus on what I have accomplished so far and plan ways to include more of your practical suggestions into my lifestyle in the year ahead. One of the most important things I took away from *52 Weeks of Tranquility* is that self-care is not selfish and in fact really needs to be a priority in my life. I've heard this before, from you and from others, but I finally "got" it. For many years, I neglected my health and well-being in service of career and other people's needs. I'm resolving to treat myself much better in the new year!

~ Sonja Barisic

Receiving *52 Weeks of Tranquility* from Kimberly Wilson each week was truly a treasure. 2015 was a bit of a challenging year for me (kids' flying from the nest, possible job relocation, major basement flood…) and I really needed some inspiration. And, I'm happy to say, it arrived weekly in the form of an email from Kimberly. Every time I opened the post and read Kimberly's tip for the week, I was inspired and moved to make a small change, practice awareness and be grateful. Whether it was a reminder to "drink my greens," encouragement to indulge in a "bed day" or to "capture beauty in life's messy moments," Kimberly offered lots of yummy suggestions for self-care and mindfulness. One of my favorite suggestions was to acquire a tub time ritual and now I regularly treat myself to a lavish bath of salts and lavender essential oils. I've been a follower of Tranquility du Jour for many years, and *52 Weeks of Tranquility* is a wonderful addition to my Tranquility collection. Whether it was the words, the inspired advice or the stunning photographs, 52 Weeks was always a welcome and required reading.

~ Linda Gallagher

52 Weeks Checklist

Use this checklist to tick off each week as you complete it and highlight your takeaways.

- ☐ Week 1: Let It Percolate _____
- ☐ Week 2: Choose Your Theme _____
- ☐ Week 3: Meditate _____
- ☐ Week 4: Clear Clutter _____
- ☐ Week 5: Sun Salute _____
- ☐ Week 6: Single-Task _____
- ☐ Week 7: Be Present _____
- ☐ Week 8: Artist's Date _____
- ☐ Week 9: Snail Mail _____
- ☐ Week 10: Try Something New _____
- ☐ Week 11: Seasonal Reflection _____
- ☐ Week 12: Your Insides _____

- ☐ Week 13: Take a Break _____
- ☐ Week 14: Get Outside _____
- ☐ Week 15: Capture the Moment _____
- ☐ Week 16: Let Go _____
- ☐ Week 17: A.M. Routine _____
- ☐ Week 18: Add Beauty _____
- ☐ Week 19: Get Away _____
- ☐ Week 20: Read _____
- ☐ Week 21: Carve Your Path _____
- ☐ Week 22: Breathe _____
- ☐ Week 23: Fleurs _____
- ☐ Week 24: Sip Tea _____

- ☐ Week 25: Eat Your Veggies _____
- ☐ Week 26: Write _____
- ☐ Week 27: Pen Month's Dreams _____
- ☐ Week 28: P.M. Routine _____
- ☐ Week 29: Mindful Eating _____
- ☐ Week 30: Practice Acceptance _____
- ☐ Week 31: Embrace Minimalism _____
- ☐ Week 32: Drink Your Greens _____
- ☐ Week 33: Walk _____
- ☐ Week 34: Signature Style _____
- ☐ Week 35: Journal _____
- ☐ Week 36: Oil Up _____
- ☐ Week 37: Soak in the Tub _____
- ☐ Week 38: Entertain _____
- ☐ Week 39: Review Budget _____
- ☐ Week 40: Volunteer _____
- ☐ Week 41: Create _____
- ☐ Week 42: Productivity _____
- ☐ Week 43: Body Scan _____
- ☐ Week 44: Self-Care _____
- ☐ Week 45: Disconnect _____
- ☐ Week 46: Bed Day _____
- ☐ Week 47: Gratitude _____
- ☐ Week 48: Move Mindfully _____
- ☐ Week 49: Practice Yin _____
- ☐ Week 50: Hollydaze _____
- ☐ Week 51: Be Kind _____
- ☐ Week 52: Reflect _____

50 Things to Experience This Year

1. _____
2. _____
3. _____
4. _____
5. _____
6. _____
7. _____
8. _____
9. _____
10. _____
11. _____
12. _____
13. _____
14. _____
15. _____
16. _____
17. _____
18. _____
19. _____
20. _____
21. _____
22. _____
23. _____
24. _____
25. _____
26. _____
27. _____
28. _____
29. _____
30. _____
31. _____
32. _____
33. _____
34. _____
35. _____
36. _____
37. _____
38. _____
39. _____
40. _____
41. _____
42. _____
43. _____
44. _____
45. _____
46. _____
47. _____
48. _____
49. _____
50. _____

24 Books to Read This Year

1. _____
2. _____
3. _____
4. _____
5. _____
6. _____
7. _____
8. _____
9. _____
10. _____
11. _____
12. _____
13. _____
14. _____
15. _____
16. _____
17. _____
18. _____
19. _____
20. _____
21. _____
22. _____
23. _____
24. _____

10 Places to Visit This Year

1. _____
2. _____
3. _____
4. _____
5. _____
6. _____
7. _____
8. _____
9. _____
10. _____

Start + Stop List

What I want more of and less of this year:

START	STOP
1.	1.
2.	2.
3.	3.
4.	4.
5.	5.
6.	6.
7.	7.
8.	8.
9.	9.
10.	10.
11.	11.
12.	12.
13.	13.
14.	14.
15.	15.
16.	16.
17.	17.
18.	18.
19.	19.
20.	20.

Gratitude List

1. _____
2. _____
3. _____
4. _____
5. _____
6. _____
7. _____
8. _____
9. _____
10. _____
11. _____
12. _____
13. _____
14. _____
15. _____
16. _____
17. _____
18. _____
19. _____
20. _____
21. _____
22. _____
23. _____
24. _____
25. _____
26. _____
27. _____
28. _____
29. _____
30. _____
31. _____
32. _____
33. _____
34. _____
35. _____
36. _____
37. _____
38. _____
39. _____
40. _____
41. _____
42. _____
43. _____
44. _____
45. _____
46. _____
47. _____
48. _____
49. _____
50. _____

Inspiration Spread

Use these pages to collage inspiration.

Attach images or words that represent how you want to show up this year.

Week 1: Let It Percolate

Ready to dream up this year's big adventures? Okay, maybe once you get through your inbox? Returning to routine after the holiday festivities can feel heavy.

No more homemade cookies covered with sprinkles, invites to festive parties, or anticipation of time off with loved ones. I find the first Monday *sans* twinkle lights to be one of my hardest days.

That's why we're beginning the 52 Weeks now—to inspire a different way of starting the new year. Slowly and intentionally.

There's no rush to set the perfect resolutions, get in shape, or figure out your life plan. Allow this year's dreams to percolate. I like to use "reflection, intention, action" as my road map for looking ahead.

REFLECTION: Take a few hours or days to reflect on highlights and lessons learned last year. Note what transpired throughout the year. Look through your journal, planner, or photos to recall forgotten adventures.

INTENTION: Upon review, what stands out as an overarching theme that you'd like to carry into this year? It may be a word, an image, a phrase, or a quote. Write it down and display it where you'll see it regularly. Use this word to assist with decision-making, planning, and beyond. Does the action you're considering align with your year's intention? If not, it may help you say "yes" or "no" with confidence.

ACTION: Settle back into a routine *sans* travel, family, and Santa. Notice what wants attention. Does your body need more movement? Sign up for yoga classes. Is your creative side feeling neglected? Spend time with your art journal. Is your home in disarray from holiday decor? Schedule a cathartic decluttering session. Take micromovements, one tiny step at a time.

Choose consciously. Create small changes. Listen deeply to longings within. Let's fill this year with experiences and give them proper time and space to percolate.

What do you feel brewing within?

Week 2: Choose Your Theme

When you reflect on what you'd like to see more of this year, is there a word, phrase, image, or quote that comes to mind?

For some, choosing the right word can feel daunting, as if they're stuck with something for an *entire year*, so it must be perfect.

That's why I like the idea of choosing a theme—something broad and fluid. Whatever you choose to work with, it can become a beacon for your day-to-day actions and decisions.

Since I've been doing this exercise, I've worked with the themes of spaciousness, simplicity, and beauty. After reusing the word "spaciousness" repeatedly for a few years, I'm delighted to share that it has become much more of a reality. It's like planting a seed of intention every single day, courtesy of attending to the theme.

The same with simplicity. I continue to focus on paring down to what is essential. Although there is much more room for growth, this theme is an umbrella for how I use my time and energy.

Beauty is something I seek to infuse in all that I do—from lighting candles in the morning to surrounding myself with fresh flowers to sealing snail mail love notes with washi tape. Beauty will remain a theme for years.

Choose a theme for the year. What is something you'd like to see infused into your days? If you truly lived your theme this year, how would things be different? Write about what this theme means to you. Describe it using your five senses.

Week 3: Meditate

Our brains are on overload from the moment we wake up until our heads hit the pillow. And for some, the mind continues throughout the night, unable to rest.

Studies show that we have 50,000-70,000 thoughts a day and 90-95% are repetitive. No wonder we're so tired!

Unfortunately, there isn't a magic pill to get quiet. It takes effort and discipline.

Our thoughts reflect our mindset. Tune in to yours this week. Keep a thought log. Notice what's replaying over and over again. Try to replace negative self-talk with words of encouragement.

One mindfulness teacher encourages the phrase "bless my heart" when we make a mistake or feel less than stellar. I find myself using it and "bless her/his/its heart" toward others when disappointed or feeling judgmental.

To curb the influx of thoughts, judgments, and inner dialogues, try getting quiet this week. Set aside ten minutes to sit in a chair or on a meditation cushion (I love my handmade damask one) with the simple intention to get quiet.

Eliminate distractions, light a candle, set your smartphone timer, and take your seat. Close your eyes and notice all the sensations you're experiencing—physically and emotionally. Then tune in to your breath. Notice it moving in and out of your nostrils. And remember, nothing else is supposed to be happening right now.

As your mind wanders, which it will continually, bring your awareness back to your breath. Over and over again. When you notice you've gotten caught in a story about the past or future, gently return to this very moment.

This practice is a training ground for focusing, single-tasking, and being present. Studies show that getting quiet through meditation decreases stress, pain, and anxiety while increasing positive emotions, memory, and parts of the brain associated with emotional regulation and self-control.

Try getting quiet a few times over the next week and write what you notice.

Week 4: Clear Clutter

In *The Life-Changing Magic of Tidying Up*, Marie Kondo writes, "As you put your house in order and decrease your possessions, you'll see what your true values are, what is really important to you in your life . . . focus instead on choosing the things that inspire joy and on enjoying life according to your own standards."

Her overarching message to observe the feelings evoked by possessions and to shed what doesn't evoke joy resonates. For years, I've challenged myself to let go of things that no longer bring pleasure—relationships, commitments, stuff.

Over the holidays I set aside a day to deep clean my 600-square-foot Pink Palace by going through drawers, closets, bins, counters, and all the nooks in between. By the end of the decluttering marathon, I have numerous bags of goodies to donate and piles of things to discard.

When I drop bags at Goodwill, I smile thinking about the items' new happy homes. Bring joy to others while you create more space in your life.

While there are many different methods, theories, and programs touting answers to our clutter issues, I encourage you to view your space with fresh eyes. How do you feel in your space? What is working? What needs a home? What's *really* in that catchall drawer, and do you still need it?

I came across a great quote by Joshua Becker of *Becoming Minimalist*, "Owning less is far more beneficial than organizing more." This sums up the beauty of clearing clutter—less stuff equals more time, energy, and space.

Start with a drawer, a shelf, or a tabletop. If you're ambitious, begin with a closet. Designate a spot for incoming papers and set up folders to organize the important ones. Ask yourself if the item brings you joy. Do you need and use the object regularly? If not, let it go and you'll feel lighter. Clear clutter this week and write about your experience.

Week 5: Sun Salute

Although the days are short in the Northern Hemisphere right now, a full-bodied flow of sun salutations will bring a dash of sunshine.

Sun salutations stretch, flex, and tone the body while also offering gratitude to the sun, calming the mind, and energizing the spirit.

These twelve poses are a flowing sequence best done on an empty stomach in the morning. Set the stage with a candle, yoga mat, and a dab of lavender oil on your wrists.

No experience needed. Move slowly and tune into a nine-minute mp3 where I walk you through the poses. Visit kimberlywilson.com/52weeks.

1. Come to mountain pose at the top of your mat. Press into all four corners of the feet and reach the crown of the head toward the heavens. Exhale and bring your hands to prayer position in front of your heart.
2. Inhale, extend your arms along your ears, and reach to the sky.
3. Exhale, trace your midline, and fold forward.
4. Inhale, step back with your right leg to a lunge. Lift onto your fingertips to create more space. Wiggle your right foot back so that your heel is directly over the ball of the foot, and gently rock forward and back.
5. Exhale, step back with your left leg to downward dog—an inverted V. Press the floor away from you.
6. Inhale, glide your shoulders over your wrists and your heels above the balls of your feet to plank pose. Feel the body pulled taut in two directions.
7. Exhale, drop your knees to the mat, bend your arms in a 90-degree angle, lower your shoulders and hips to a straight line while hugging your elbows to your body for half-chaturanga.
8. Inhale, uncurl your toes, drop your belly, lift your heart center, and slide into cobra. Relax your shoulders from your ears.
9. Exhale, curl your toes under, and lift your hips up and back to downward dog.
10. Inhale, step forward with your right foot. Gently rock forward and back to awaken your hips.
11. Exhale, step your left foot in between both hands to a forward fold.
12. Inhale, trace your midline as you extend the arms along your ears and reach for the sun.

Rinse and repeat for a total of five times on each side.

Try a daily sun salute this week and note the results of your practice. How do you feel before and after? How do you feel during the day? If you practice sun salutes at different times of the day, how does it affect your experience?

Week 6: Single-Task

Most days, I find myself surrounded by a journal, *Daybook*, laptop, phone, books, and multiple writing tools. Rarely will I sit down with a clear desk *sans* distractions.

For years, I responded to emails as they came in and felt chained to my computer. Before Wi-Fi and smartphones, I didn't want to leave the house to work because I'd miss an email. Sigh.

I often juggle between multiple windows in my browser (confession: currently there are 10 open) as if watching a Ping-Pong match. This can make my head spin. Relate?

More confessions: when I find myself with a spare moment in an elevator or at a stoplight, I sometimes reach for my phone. It's a nasty habit and one I'm intentionally working to shift.

When studies began coming out highlighting how multi-tasking makes us dumber, I tried to shift my tune.

David Rock, author of *Your Brain at Work*, shares that "a study done at the University of London found that constant emailing and text-messaging reduces mental capability by an average of 10 points on an IQ test. This effect is similar to missing a night's sleep. For men, it's around three times more than the effect of smoking cannabis. While this fact might make an interesting dinner party topic, it's really not that amusing that one of the most common 'productivity tools' can make one as dumb as a stoner."

Wow. Thus my transition toward trying to single-task. Charles Dickens wrote, "He did each single thing as if he did nothing else." That's a powerful blend of mindfulness, profound awareness, focus, and attention. All this helps lead to tranquility.

This week, focus on the person or task in front of you as if it was the most important thing on earth. When you feel the twinge to check your email or resort to the Facebook News Feed scroll, take a deep breath, and come back to the project at hand. Designate time for social media, task switching, and email versus letting impulse control you.

This is one of my dreams for the year and it may be a complete reconfiguration for many of us. Try single-tasking and write about the experience.

Week 7: Be Present

One weekend we drove 20 hours round-trip to take our dog, Louis, to a white sandy beach in Jacksonville, Florida. We played fetch on the beach until he lost interest, toted him around Hanna Park in a basket affixed to Tim's bike, and enjoyed a makeshift picnic with his favorite things—clementines, watermelon, and sugar snap peas.

You may have known Louis over the years. He was a nearly 10.5-year-old black pug who had been the light of our lives, lovingly placed on three of my book covers. His antics filled my social media feeds. Then he was diagnosed with terminal cancer and given a few months to live. Once we moved through the shock—complete with days in bed, lots of chocolaty comfort food, and tears—we began scheming how to make the most of his final days.

While we were in Florida soaking up the sun, we started planning another trip south. Discussing logistics as the waves lapped up, we expressed dismay at focusing on our next adventure and missing the current one. It was one of those aha moments where you realize you're completely missing the experience you're in by looking ahead.

Mindfulness, according to Jon Kabat-Zinn, is defined as "paying attention in the moment, with awareness, on purpose, non-judgmentally." In that moment, we caught ourselves, had a laugh about our lack of presence in such a perfect setting, and returned to focus on what was in front of us—white sand, blue water, and a frolicking pug.

It's easy to get caught in that cycle. You know, rehashing the past or dreaming about the future and missing the moment.

Being in that situation—striving to make the most of what little time we have left with a beloved member of our family—was a constant call back to presence. The good news is that you don't need a life-or-death-situation to make that happen. Start with the awareness and discipline to return to the moment when you find you've strayed. Again and again.

Crafting to-dos, replaying old hurts, or pondering what's missing prevents us from living our lives. This week, when you're with a loved one, in a meeting, or driving home, notice how often the mind moves out of the moment and see if you can bring yourself back to the now.

Week 8: Artist's Date

Julia Cameron, author of the life-changing book *The Artist's Way*, coined Artist's Dates—a one-hour weekly solo excursion to nurture your creative spark. The key is to spend time with your inner artist.

This adventure gives the mind the opportunity to rest, play, and uncover ideas that may not be heard in daily life.

I've been an avid fan of the idea for nearly two decades and strive to include it in my weekly routine. Spontaneously as I pass a bookstore, or planned as I sign up for a calligraphy workshop.

Sitting at home surrounded by reading materials (*Flow* and *Bella Grace* magazines are my current favorites), my journal, markers, a lit candle, and a cuppa tea stirs my soul. If I'm feeling adventurous, I gather these tools and head to a *café*. A new setting offers a sense of spaciousness and change of scenery to muse and dream.

A few ideas for Artist's Date include:

- Sit at a *café* and pen your thoughts
- Visit a museum during your lunch hour
- Pick up supplies at a craft store
- Browse in a bookstore
- Wander the aisles of an art store
- Take a calligraphy class
- Visit an animal sanctuary or shelter
- Plant herbs in terracotta pots on your windowsill
- Picnic with a juicy book
- Try ice skating
- People-watch in a park
- Stroll with no intended destination
- Enjoy a matinee
- Pull out your journal and creativity tools
- Hit the library
- Start a blog
- Send a care package
- Write a letter to your future self
- Lose yourself in a thrift store
- Ride a train round-trip without a planned destination
- Read an old journal
- Play tourist in your town

You may think, "I don't have time for this, I can barely handle groceries, laundry, and pet care!" Make time for it, because this practice will fuel your soul. Try incorporating a stop at an art store while you're out running errands. Pause at a park while walking your dog to write in your journal. Carry a coloring book and use it to de-stress when picking up your afternoon latte.

In *Tranquility du Jour* podcast #313, author Sam Bennett encouraged listeners to fill their teacup and share the overflow with others (versus giving all of ourselves and having nothing left). This visual has served as the perfect metaphor for self-care, personal development, and Artist's Dates.

This week, take one hour for yourself. Gather a few creative tools and go to a new spot you've wanted to try. Settle in and write about what unfolds. This tool is a sacred gift from you to you.

Week 9: Snail Mail

With email, text messaging, and online chats, snail mail has lost popularity. Yet sitting down with pen and paper to write a letter connects us to a quaint pastime.

Each time I pick up mail and see a handwritten address on the envelope, a smile washes over my face. It means a treat is inside.

Over the years I've created a basket of stationery supplies that elevate the practice of penning a love note to an Artist's Date.

Pulling out a sheet of patterned paper to write a thank you or thinking-of-you note is an intimate tool for connection beyond the Internet. It's a visual, tactile experience for both the sender and receiver. Adding lavender buds or a fragrant tea bag makes it a "scentual" experience.

According to Simon Garfield, author of *To the Letter: A Celebration of the Lost Art of Letter Writing*, "Emails are a poke, but letters are a caress, and letters stick around to be newly discovered." Caress someone you love with your handwritten words.

Not sure where to start? Think of someone who has given you a gift, supported you in some way, or may need a jolt of encouragement. Grab your tools and express yourself. Your love note may simply be a few sentences penned with a Sharpie onto a blank card. That may be all that is needed to make someone's day.

Stuff a love note inside your child's lunch box or your partner's messenger bag. Leave a "good job" note on a colleague's desk. Pen a thank you for a lesson learned or gift received. Create a handmade birthday card complete with the recipient's initials in glass glitter.

Supplies are minimal. Browse Paper Source, Etsy, Tarjay's stationery aisle, or discount stores such as T.J.Maxx. Choose blank note cards that reflect your spirit and can be used for numerous occasions.

Pick up a sheet of stamps and keep a few favorite flowy pens in your purse and on your desk (my go-to is the Paper Mate Flair). Invest in an address stamp or personalized labels that reflect your personality. Add a strip of colorful washi tape or a fancy wax seal to close the envelope. These are all the tools you need to bring a smile to someone's face.

This week, reach out to a friend with a thoughtful note to let them know they're on your mind and you're sending good thoughts. Include a bag of tea, article of interest, or handmade token. This sweet gesture goes a long way in our fast-paced society.

Week 10: Try Something New

After a struggle-filled start (complete with trying to pay an online bill and locking myself out of the system while Louis "burfed" at me repeatedly, wanting something I was unable to decipher), I hopped in an Uber at a huge snow surcharge and headed to meet a friend for brunch.

By the time I arrived I was teary, frustrated with myself, and wanted to crawl back into bed to curl up in the fetal position.

After a cuppa jasmine tea, a few tears, and niceties exchanged with a friend, I felt my body soften and shift into anticipation of a workshop we'd been looking forward to for three months: calligraphy.

The first few exercises were basic guideline drawings followed by line drawings. I felt my frustration returning. I wasn't a natural. Then we turned to squiggle letters like u and n.

Again, frustration and tears were building. It was me returning to 7th grade class (I still recall the desk's placement in the room 30 years later) trying to comprehend algebra and hearing my teacher "wah wah wah" over and over again.

Somehow I put on my big-girl-pants and kept trying. I mean, I wanted to learn, I'd set aside 3.5 hours to do so, and I needed to shift these dreaded feelings. We were moving on to the lowercase alphabet. Uh oh, I needed a green tea refill for this one. I watched in awe as she demonstrated with ease.

Upon returning to my spot at the table, I diligently practiced A-Z in lowercase. You'll see examples of my name, Paris, yoga, macaron, and kale in the above image. Again, I felt my body softening along with the negative self-talk and I got lost in the flow.

Next she had us gather for the final demonstration of uppercase letters, touted as easier. When she stated that those whose name began with the letter "K" had many style options, I somehow felt ahead of the game. "Yay, something in my favor today!"

She was right. Uppercase letters were a teeny tiny bit easier. I'd struggled with the basic strokes for so long that I was beginning to get the hang of it.

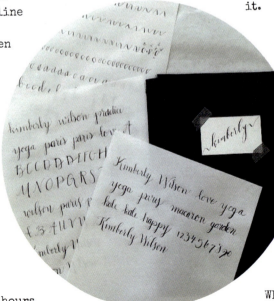

The workshop ended with her writing our names (you'll see the perfect version at the bottom of the top sheet) so that we could see how to connect the letters we'd practiced all morning.

I left feeling empowered and eager to continue practicing with my new tools (ink, pen, nibs, and paper). It took some moxie to get to this stage, considering the day's start and my frustration with being an oh-so-challenged beginner.

While there are many fits and starts to

trying something new, I value the possibility. Sure, we may not be a natural (and happen to be sitting across from a graphic designer at the calligraphy class, no pressure!) or may find that the thing we've tried isn't what we'd hoped for. However, we tried!

To find passions, we need to keep exploring, deepening, and growing. Why stick with one style of yoga? Why just one way of writing a letter? Why the same Artist's Date week after week? Sure, there is something beautiful in routine, but there is something equally poetic in moving beyond the comfort zone.

Week 11: Seasonal Reflection

Those of us in the Northern Hemisphere are being led into the spring equinox. After winters filled with snow days, heavy boots, and ice storms, there is deep anticipation for spring blooms.

As barren trees transform to green, tulips push from parched soil, and cherry blossoms pop up along Washington, D.C.'s Tidal Basin, I, too, experience the gentle nudge to move out of hibernation.

During this seasonal shift, I like to sit down with a pen and paper to reflect on how I'm feeling about the activities that populate my days. Set aside at least 30 minutes to consider how you're feeling in each broad category of your life.

Set the stage for your reflection. Light a candle, turn on inspiring tunes (may I recommend Pink Martini?), pour a bubbly libation, grab your journal and writing tools, and settle in for reflection. Make it an experience.

There may be some categories you're drawn to and others that don't fully resonate. Choose an assortment of at least eight to give a holistic big picture.

Consider these categories:

Work
Style
Creativity
Dreams
Giving back
Home
Self-Care
Mindfulness
Spirituality
Finances
Education
Relationships
Romance
Family
Fitness
Self-Love
Health
Parenting

Rate them on overall satisfaction using a scale of 1-10 (1 not at all satisfied, 5 neutral, 10 incredibly satisfied).

When ranking, approach this as you would a multiple-choice test and go with your initial gut reaction. Answers will vary based on what you're currently

experiencing. For example, recent receipt of a large bill may lead to a lower finances score than usual.

Observe your ratings and notice one or two that appear closer to *your* (not society's) definition of a perfect 10. Yes, even a six counts as high! Give yourself kudos and raise a glass in honor of your efforts.

Next, note areas that are lower than you'd like them to be and pen a few action steps for growth.

For example, if creativity ranked lower than you'd like, consider ways to infuse more creativity into your daily life. Try a new recipe, take a watercolor class, or walk your dog on a new morning route.

If you'd like to increase do-gooding, look for volunteer opportunities in your community, start a monthly donation to a favorite charity, or make an effort to compliment one person each day.

Use this process every three months as a way to reconnect with your BIG picture. Acknowledge progress while noting where you may have slightly strayed off course.

Week 12: Your Insides, Another's Outsides

Have you ever found yourself scrolling through Facebook, Instagram, or Pinterest looking at someone else's life and feeling bad about your own? Guilty as charged.

There are darling pics of blowing glitter, weddings under the Eiffel Tower, precious Pottery Barn nurseries, or elegant dinner parties filled with beautiful people.

Of course, the glitter cleanup, heated wedding planning discussions, diaper changings, burnt *entrée*, and flaky friendships are often left out of our social media feeds.

And for good reason. Who wants to see that, right? We have enough burnt *entrées* in our own lives. Social media is a form of fantasy, a peek into another's limited reality, and an escape from our own.

In former days, we used annual holiday letters and in-person gatherings to share our exploits and tell stories about how smart little Johnny was becoming. Now we can post these updates across many platforms, multiple times a day.

This isn't a "social media is bad" essay, but rather a reminder that what we share publicly is a snippet of reality. Typically the most favorable scene possible, with a bit of photo editing and clever comments thrown in.

For example, this family selfie was taken at the Washington Humane Society's Sugar and Champagne event. When we posted the pictures from our evening on Instagram and Facebook, we received many sweet comments about how happy and healthy Louis looked.

Ironically, a week before he was diagnosed with terminal brain cancer and we debated whether we should still go. We were only a couple of weeks away from his terrifying grand mal seizure and living in constant fear of another seizure.

Also, his "smiling" came from eating every doggie treat possible and being in a continual state of panting due to his medications and condition.

While we loved the kind words about how he looked, we also knew the truth. And so does everyone else posting a pretty, happy picture or update online.

Remember, you see one side of the full, complicated adventure that is someone else's life. Before coveting another's exploits, style, or perfectly decorated home, try looking around at your own beautifully knotty life.

You know about the items thrown into a corner to hide clutter for that living room shot and the multiple takes it took to get that perfect family photo. Comparing your insides to another person's outsides is a recipe for disappointment.

Reality is filled with the beautiful mess of everyday life. Burnt *entrées* and all.

This week, observe how social media affects how you feel.

Week 13: Take a Break

On a sunny, 70-degree day, I was in a windowless conference room learning new therapy techniques. After biking home from the psychotherapy conference, I headed inside and declared, "We *must* get outside now!"

I had an hour to spare before my next appointment and felt strongly it needed to be used wisely and intentionally.

Louis had taken a strong decline, so I was eager to connect with him and Tim while savoring vitamin D.

We debated between a bike ride, a quick picnic, a walk to Dupont Circle. Louis was in no mood for long travels, so around the corner we went to take full advantage of those precious 60 minutes (see pic below). Ah, a break.

A few days later, I returned home withered from the conference. Despite it being 6 p.m., it was naptime. After shedding a few layers, I crawled into bed guilt-free and awoke refreshed shortly thereafter.

Life has a way of keeping us in constant movement. Bills to be paid, meals to be made, taxes to be done, kids to be fed, laundry to be washed, and on and on. Yet it's the magic within these mundane moments that can transform.

At the conference, I had the opportunity to study again with mindfulness teacher Jon Kabat-Zinn, and he shared that Oprah had recently asked him if there was life after death. He responded that he was more interested in whether there was life *before* death.

He went on to share a favorite quote by Henry David Thoreau, "I went to the woods because I wished to live deliberately, to front only the essential facts of life, and see if I could not learn what it had to teach, and not, when I came to die, discover that I had not lived."

As you move forward this week, create and savor open pockets of time and space.

This may come in the form of a cuppa tea, a walk around the block, a nap, a few minutes of reading in the park during your lunch break, or a few deep breaths while waiting in line at the grocery store.

Know that these moments aren't indulgent, but rather necessary for soul survival. So, dear one, take a much-deserved break this week and write about your experience.

Week 14: Get Outside

After a fairly tumultuous week, we packed up and headed for a weekend in the hills. Desperately craving tranquility, open schedules, and fresh air, a trip to Shenandoah National Park was the perfect balm.

Both days we hiked with Louis in tow and hit dog-friendly wineries. Sipping a Virginia white wine mid-afternoon felt decadent. And necessary.

On the trail, I took note of the little things. The crackling leaves beneath each step. The smell of pine and nearby campfires. Louis' deep breath and excited gallop. Sweet purple wildflowers growing near an emerald-colored fern. A nearby stream rippling over the rocks.

Considering how cooped up we'd been due to a long, cold Northeast winter, the feel of sunshine on our skin and the crisp mountain air was a welcome dose of nature therapy.

Nature helps put things in perspective. My tiny mishaps and frustrations from the previous week began to lighten.

Albert Einstein said, "Look deep into nature, and then you will understand everything better." I've found this to be true.

Studies show that direct contact with nature increases mental health and spiritual development. Benefits include stress reduction, heightened creativity, and a broader sense of interconnectedness.

John Muir said, "Climb the mountains and get their good tidings. Nature's peace will flow into you as sunshine flows into trees. The winds will blow their own freshness into you … while cares will drop off like autumn leaves." And that, dear reader, is my wish for you.

This week, infuse a dose of vitamin N (vitamin Nature) in your day. Get off the Metro one stop away from your destination and savor the walk to work. Stroll through the city during your lunch break. Take your dog for a walk in a nearby park. Bike to your next meeting. Consider a picnic with your beloved or bestie.

Week 15: Capture the Moment

Famed photographer Ansel Adams said that you don't take a photograph, you make it.

For as long as I can remember, photography has been part of my life. While I was growing up, my father had his own darkroom and we regularly received new point-and-shoot film cameras for the holidays (after posing by the tree AND with each gift, of course).

I spent more time "modeling" on rocks in the mountains than most kids spent playing in the sandbox.

Although I've never had a fancy camera (the instruction manuals make me cry), I use my iPhone to capture sweet moments of every day. I took an iPhoneography class a few years ago and was introduced to many editing apps.

Yet the basic iPhone camera and tools in Instagram tend to be my go-to. Simple. And no instruction manual needed.

One spring day we gathered Louis for a morning among the cherry blossoms before the swarm of tourists descended. I captured this shot of the Jefferson Memorial and Tidal Basin framed by peaked blooms. Although I had to zoom heavily (contributing to a grainy look) and dodge the increasing crowd, I love the way it turned out.

This week, carry a camera or your smartphone and capture inspiration in the moment. Observe a bathing bird, a tree in bloom, a cuppa steaming tea, sunlit a patch of grass, or a colorful pair of shoes in a window (or on your feet). Snap it!

Need a few tips to exercise your photography muscles? Here are my basics:

- Avoid auto flash and look for natural lighting. Snap in the golden hours—shortly after sunrise or before sunset.
- Crop photos when shooting versus spending lots of time in post-production editing.
- Frame your images with overhanging branches.
- Zoom in to capture details.
- Use props such as chalkboards, flowers, baskets, yoga mats, bicycles, umbrellas, books, vintage suitcases, quilts.
- Avoid direct sunlight = distracting shadows.
- Remove clutter like cords or pet toys from the shot.

- Snap unique personal details (journals, art supplies, tea mug).
- Use fun backgrounds such as painted brick walls, murals, and wood fences.

Above all, have fun and pay attention to the beautiful (and messy) details of daily life.

Week 16: Let Go

The past few years have been filled with immense loss. From losing my beloved Gramma, to my firstborn rescue kitty, to my constant canine companion Louis. This photo was taken on our last walk together.

Loss is a part of our lives—unemployment, friendships, breakups, moves, illness, and death.

I turned to my loss go-to book, *Grieving Mindfully* by Sameet M. Kumar, Ph.D. One passage stood out and felt like a good reminder:

"Although loss often makes you feel as if a door has closed on a relationship, in time you will see that actually a new door has opened—one that leads to the rest of your life."

This passage was a necessary boost on an otherwise dreary day. And it led me to reflect on the mantra "let go."

Yoga teacher Sharon Gannon of Jivamutki Yoga introduced this mantra to me. Inhale and silently say, "Let." Exhale and silently say, "Go." It's simple, focuses the mind, and it works.

Letting go is about dealing with loss, expectations, uncertainty, and beyond.

Jon Kabat-Zinn says, "To let go means to give up coercing, resisting, or struggling, in exchange for something more powerful and wholesome which comes out of allowing things to be as they are without getting caught up in your attraction to or rejection of them, in the intrinsic stickiness of wanting, of liking and disliking."

Grasping or trying to hold on to things as we want them to be (youth, health, weather, traffic) leads to disappointment.

This doesn't mean we don't love other beings or long for great things. It simply means we release our attachment to them being a certain way. We show up with great love and dreams, then let go of the outcome. And let them, or us, fly.

Spend a moment reflecting this week on any of the things you're holding onto that may not serve you (job, location, relationships, expectations, commitments, dreams). Then consider whether this is the time to begin the process of letting them go.

For me, periods of grief mean letting go of numerous commitments in my *Daybook* and lessening expectations around what needs to get done. The process of mourning takes top priority.

Week 17: A.M. Routine

For a decade, my go-to morning routine involved catering to Louis' needs, which always revolved around food. The first week without him was eerily quiet and required reframing. Although it felt hollow without a dog circling my feet and demanding breakfast, it was a nudge toward a new routine.

Numerous studies point to the importance of using a morning routine (or ritual, if you prefer) to set yourself up for success. Laura Vanderkam (*Tranquility du Jour* podcasts #199, #263, #306, #343) researched many morning routines and wrote *What the Most Successful People Do Before Breakfast*. She points out that waking up early and exercising is a top priority among successful, productive people.

Often referred to as the "Golden Hour," the time when you wake up is considered a precious opportunity to begin anew after sleep has cleared your brain. Julia Cameron, author of *The Artist's Way*, recommends writing Morning Pages (three pages of longhand, stream of consciousness pages writing) first thing for this very reason.

The goal is to create a routine that becomes as habitual as brushing your teeth. The more decisions one has to make, the more brainpower is used. Also, studies show we have more self-control in the morning, so why not use it to your advantage? By creating an energizing and inspiring routine, you can move through it without having to overthink.

Ever have someone ask you a question early in the morning and it's just too much to process? It often happens to me when I ask Tim something before he's had his coffee. We need time to wake up and nourish our spirit without puttering this time away. Does scrolling through Facebook's News Feed or diving into email sound familiar? Guilty as charged (especially when tired).

Begin the day with your "big rocks" (coined in *7 Habits of Highly Effective People* as your priorities) or M.I.T. (Most Important Tasks) to focus on projects that take the most brainpower. Make time for a personal passion first thing to ensure it happens. Leave it until after a day job and you may be too tired to write, garden, paint, or move forward with a dream, which can feel defeating.

My ideal morning routine includes hot water with lemon, 10 minutes of yoga, five minutes of meditation, journal writing, a green juice or smoothie, and a review of the day's agenda. Then comes email, writing, or dashing out to appointments, ideally refreshed and satiated.

Picture your ideal morning. How does it begin? At what time? Whom are you with? What are your practices? What do you consume—food, drink, media? This week, play with different combinations of activities and note what works for you. Shift what doesn't. Open yourself to possibility.

May your morning routine align with your values and set the framework for forward motion in the direction of your dreams. Making tiny shifts can have a profound impact on your overall day, mood, and productivity.

Week 18: Add Beauty

When hosting an Art + Yoga retreat in West Virginia, I encourage reflection on what creativity is and how it shows up in the participants' lives.

Surprisingly, creativity can be a hard concept to define despite it being a household word for many. According to Webster's dictionary, creativity is the ability to make new things or think of new ideas.

One participant shared how she incorporates creativity by adding beauty, and the veils were lifted. A light bulb seemed to go off—adding beauty to one's every day. Of course, *that's* creativity.

I love to exercise my creative muscles by setting up for these retreats: fluffing tissue paper pom-poms, arranging flowers, stringing handmade bunting and twinkle lights, labeling Mason jars with washi tape, burning scented candles, inserting striped paper straws into glasses, placing doilies under dishware, taking great care in wrapping and displaying their goody bags. Adding beauty becomes art.

No need to save adding beauty for retreats. Sprinkle it into your every day life. When sitting down for a meal, light candles, use the good china, and turn off the TV. Savor each bite and honor the food's journey to your plate.

For example, when practicing mindful eating with a raisin, you're encouraged to reflect on the raisin's journey from a grape on the vine to your plate, and to offer gratitude to all who made it possible—including the sun (see Week 29: Mindful Eating).

Add beauty when getting ready for the day. Savor the sensations of water on your skin, lather yourself in sweet almond oil, choose your favorite outfit, add an accessory or two, coat your eyelashes with mascara and your lips with gloss, and spritz your favorite parfum.

At work, top your desk with a bouquet of flowers or an easy-to-care-for plant, and add a recycled tin can filled with colored pens, a framed photo, art postcard, or quote to inspire. Have tranquility tools tucked into your desk drawer or purse: lavender oil, travel candle and matches, raw almonds, crystallized lemon or grapefruit packets, tea bags, earplugs, argan oil, and lip gloss.

Consider your daily activities. How can you add beauty to them? What feels rote and could benefit from a splash of love? This week, infuse your moments—which make up your days, years, lifetime—with beauty and watch your creativity bloom.

Week 19: Get Away

A change of scenery can reap great benefits.

One Saturday morning I packed up my gold tote and headed to the train station bound for New York City. During the four-hour ride, Tim and I read, shared photos of available rescue dogs, and gazed out the window.

We had spontaneously planned this trip two weeks earlier, noting that we needed a new setting where we could be entertained and not have to be "on."

Tim had train travel points and I had a free place to stay, so we splurged on a few luxuries—high tea at The Plaza, *An American in Paris* on Broadway, and walks through the High Line and Central Park (where this photo was snapped).

While I'm a proponent of creating routines that set us up for success, I've also come to recognize the value in doing things differently from time to time. Stepping out of the day-to-day minutiae may offer the chance to exhale and regroup.

A 30-hour whirlwind jaunt to the Big Apple may not interest you, so let's explore additional options to get away. During mini breaks between clients, I'll often take a walk around the block to savor a dose of vitamin D or sit in a *café* and sip an iced green tea while penning snail mail.

Your definition of a getaway may be a family beach vacation, a solo sojourn to a cabin in the woods, or an afternoon picnic in the park. The *type* of getaway isn't as important—it's personal, based on familial and work obligations plus budget and time. Make it yours.

Step outside the norm and be swept into a new vista. Small shake-ups enhance our creativity, offer us the opportunity to reflect and renew outside of our daily to-dos, and create a ripple effect of well-being.

Take a peek at your calendar and add in an hour or more getaway of your choosing. It may be outside, in a museum, or in a faraway retreat center. The location isn't important. It's all about the intention behind getting away that creates the opportunity for growth.

Shift your routine slightly this week to offer a change in perspective and fresh view.

Week 20: Read

For years, I've looked to books for answers and found my heart racing with anticipation as I step into a bookstore, library, or bookstore of a boutique (hello, Anthropologie).

Bookstores promise the opportunity to gain new knowledge, enhance my life in some way, or better understand the human psyche by reading others' stories.

A recent Artist's Date was the film *Iris*, which captures one senior woman's funky signature style. Feeling inspired, I headed to the nearby Barnes and Noble to lose myself in the magical two-level sanctuary.

I didn't buy a thing due to my overflowing to-read pile, but I made my rounds through the blank journals, magazines, business, memoir, and writing books. Before I knew it, my allotted time was up.

Determined to shake things up, the next day I headed to a *café* with *My Year with Eleanor: A Memoir* in hand, sipped an effervescent San Pellegrino, and lost myself in another's world. This offered a respite within the weekend's to-dos. Books give us that gift.

One night I propped my clogs onto a damask ottoman, nestled into the settee with two black cats, and finished *The Glitter Plan*. Considering I find myself reading multiple (like 50) books at a time, finishing one calls for some sort of celebration. Pop the bubbly!

Book-buying has become an addiction of sorts over the years (leading to a few self-induced moratoriums), yet I can't shake my love of the written word. Writers bare their souls and offer readers the opportunity to learn, grow, grieve, create, and/or be inspired along with them—sometimes all in one book.

One of my books, *Tranquilologie*, lists various daily, weekly, and monthly Tranquility Tools and encourages reading two books per month. While there's no golden number, 24 books a year feels doable and still ambitious.

Since joining Goodreads, I've found changing a book from "to-read" to "read" satisfying. For me, it's like receiving a gold star—something more than the blue participation ribbon.

When you find yourself scrolling through Facebook or watching TV because you're too tired to redirect your attention or need a reality escape, grab a book and create an experience. Light candles, fix a favorite libation, settle into a comfy nook, and get lost in text beyond what your Facebook friend is upset about or eating for dinner.

Need accountability to make it happen? Create a book group with a few like-hearted ladies, contribute to an online book club, or join a platform like Goodreads where you can track your reading habits.

This week, make a list of books you're currently reading and books you want to read. Schedule time in your planner to get through one of these books and strive to make reading a habit. Tote a book (or e-reader) with you at all times—you never know when there will be a few free minutes and you can get deeper into that juicy novel.

Week 21: Carve Your Path

Enveloped by lush foliage and singing birds en route to a 7 a.m. yoga class, I felt deep gratitude for having chosen a different path.

Nearly 15 years ago I did the unthinkable and quit my full-time job with health insurance and a 401K to pursue teaching yoga full-time.

This was before Christy Turlington graced the cover of *Time* magazine doing yoga. Before neighborhoods (even cities) had yoga studios within reach. Before I had any data beyond a gut instinct that I could become an entrepreneur.

Honestly, I'm not even sure I knew what an entrepreneur was or that it was French! I simply knew it was time to pursue opportunities outside of a fluorescent-lit cubicle.

2015 marked my 10th time teaching yoga in Costa Rica. When I set out on this self-employment journey in 2000, I never dreamed it would lead me to such exotic places or to connect with such beautiful souls. Repeatedly.

Growing up in Oklahoma, *exotic* was a trip to the Oklahoma City mall—an entire two-hour journey from my hometown to the big city. As you may imagine, my definition has evolved dramatically over the years.

Choosing a different path from what seems sensible, aligned with your family's (or society's) expectations, or the direction you've been heading, can be scary. Even isolating.

If I hadn't given my two-week notice in my mid-twenties, I wouldn't be hosting retreats in Costa Rica. I'd probably be processing higher-profile trademarks for large corporations, managing accounts, and wondering if there was more to life.

I'm here to tell you, there is more.

While I know my journey is not for everyone and I don't dare believe I have all the answers, I do know that carving my own scary, winding, and at times muddy path has given my Oklahoma-rooted life meaning. And passport stamps.

When we step off the hamster wheel, we may be met with sorrow because we no longer recognize ourselves. Or who we once were has withered and died. Or that we hadn't heard that deep longing to change course because we were too busy.

Take a moment this week to reflect on your path. Have you chosen the path less or well-traveled? How's it working for you? Do you see an alluring fork in the road? Is there a clearing up ahead promising open space to try something new?

Sometimes the course change is as simple as a new addition to your morning routine or another shade of lipstick. Other times it may involve setting clear boundaries, adjusting expectations, or going on an Artist's Date. Or it may be a bold change in your career, relationship, living situation, or education.

Carve your own path and know there's a community for you. It may be winding, but it's worth the twists and turns.

Week 22: Breathe

The pilot warned us that there may be a few bumps during the three-hour flight, but I wasn't fully prepared for the plane's sway.

As usual, I settled into my window seat, pulled out a book and water bottle, popped in earplugs, and buckled the seat belt.

I was a late bloomer—not stepping onto a plane until high school. My parents preferred to drive cross-country for adventures. During my first flight, I was mesmerized with floating through the air and watching clouds pass by.

That fascination didn't last long. I quickly developed an intense fear of flying. When a pilot mentions that there may be a few bumps, I become less than tranquil. And this flight left me agitated.

As we oscillated, I looked around the plane and everyone else seemed to be happily engrossed in a book or a nap. Not me—despite having Jon Kabat-Zinn's mindfulness tome, *Full Catastrophe Living*, on my lap. During one particularly strong bout of turbulence, I gripped the seat in front of me to steady myself as my heart raced.

It was then that I turned to my breath. Time to call on the years of yoga training. Inhale, exhale. Repeat. Again and again.

After a few rounds of full breaths, I returned to a state of equilibrium and luckily so did the plane. I was able to stop clutching my neighbor's seat and settle back into my book on Mindfulness-Based Stress Reduction. Oh, the irony.

Our breath has the capacity to heal and ground us. The best part—it's at the ready. Always willing to serve.

My go-to breath practice is the three-part yogic breath. Here's how it works: Inhale deeply through your nose. Bring the breath into your belly, ribs, and chest. Exhale through your nose, feel the breath release from the chest, ribs, and belly. Repeat at least 10 times, and watch the tension fade away.

If you're not sure the breath is making its way to these three parts, place your hands on your belly to see if it's moving in and out. Then your ribs, and finally the sternum.

Our typical breath tends to be short and shallow and generate from the chest, so you'll probably notice that the belly breath is the hardest to find. This breath is a balm for your nervous system.

This week, when you find yourself in a challenging meeting, the recipient of a frustrating email, or on a long commute, pause and practice this breath. No one knows what you're doing, so you don't have to excuse yourself.

You can stay right in the midst of the drama and find a sense of inner peace, one breath at a time.

Week 23: Fleurs

Picking up peonies was a top priority upon arrival in Paris, so we hit the Montparnasse farmers' market first thing.

After scooping up cherries, strawberries, croissants, olives, lettuce, an olive baguette, avocados, cherry tomatoes, and peonies, we had our Parisian necessities in hand.

"I must have flowers, always and always," Claude Monet declared. I agree.

Although freshly-cut flowers may feel frivolous to some, studies show that they enhance our well-being (as if we needed a study for this, but hey, some people like data).

According to the website *Florist Chronicles*, a behavioral research study reveals that people feel more compassionate toward others, have less worry and anxiety, and feel less depressed when freshly-cut flowers are present in the home.

Need more data? Leatrice Eiseman, Executive Director of the Pantone Color Institute, states, "Our response to color is intensely emotional, and flowers can be a catalyst for feelings that stimulate more than just our senses of sight and smell. An artful floral arrangement has the ability to convey a feeling or create a mood without using words, just color."

When passing a flower stand, what do you notice? I'm drawn in with a deep appreciation for the intricate beauty of the tiny petals and the calming colors.

Our rented Paris apartment had a tiny communal garden filled with vibrant flowers and a light-colored pebble walkway—the contrast highlights the bright pink and purple hues. With each entry and exit through this space, a smile washed over my face. I mean, how could it not?

This week, treat yourself to a favorite flower. Maybe it's one clipping from your backyard garden, a few stems of lilies from a farmers' market, or an assorted bouquet from a sidewalk stand.

Notice the effect. Does your home or office feel more inviting? How does your mood shift? What colors or scents are you drawn to?

Flowers are one of nature's many works of art, and what a blessing to be able to display one on a kitchen table or brighten up a fluorescent-lit cubicle!

Week 24: Sip Tea

Green tea with rose petals and mint. Black tea with marigold and cornflower. White tea with violet petals. The options are endless.

During the Penning in Paris retreat, I hit Angelina's, Ladurée, and many sidewalk cafés for a yummy cup of exotic tea blends.

This image captures my final pot of *le thé vert à la menthe* (mint green tea) consumed before heading to the airport. I savored it slowly, paying special attention to the hints of flavor resting on my tongue before sliding down my throat.

Sipping tea can be a mindfulness practice, an opportunity to slow down. Zen Buddhist monk Thich Nhat Hahn teaches, "Drink your tea slowly and reverently, as if it is the axis on which the world revolves—slowly, evenly, without rushing toward the future. Live the actual moment. Only this moment is life."

The consumption of tea is simple, yet has many sensory-filled steps. Connect to your breath. Create an intention for the day, for the moment, or for the time it takes to consume your cup of tea. Heat the water. Listen to it boil. Choose your pleasure: grassy, fruity, flowery, blooming.

Pour the water over your tea and listen to it hit the bottom of the cup.

Let it steep for two to five minutes depending on the type of tea. Smell the aroma of your chosen infusion. Feel the warm cup in your hands. Observe the steam rising. Taste the tea in your mouth. Swish it around. Note the flavors. Then feel the heat as it flows into your body.

You don't need any fancy equipment—simply a mug, hot water, tea. And time. Time to be present and to tune in to your senses.

If you're a coffee person, the same process applies. Rather than gulping it down en route to your next meeting, feel the warmth, take in the aromas, and enjoy its time in your mouth.

This week, create a ritual out of your libation. Take time making it. Put it in a fancy mug. Sit down with the beverage and sip it like a fine wine. Connect to your breath and notice what comes up as you slow down.

Week 25: Eat Your Veggies

Bitter. Sweet. Crunchy. Chewy. Greens. Yellows. Reds. Whites. Oranges. Crispy. Mushy. Baked. Fried.

They come in all shapes, sizes, tastes, and textures. Welcome to the wild, wild world of veggies.

This photo was snapped at a farmers' market in Paris where the colorful assortment drew me in.

Choosing more plant-based options benefits not only your health, but also the environment and the animals. You know I'm like crazy obsessed with pigs, right?

Guess America's most consumed veggie? Yep, the potato. *Bonjour* French fries!

Although my sweet tooth has controlled me since infancy, I find there is something satisfying about a huge spinach salad topped with strawberry and apple slices, blueberries, grape tomatoes, walnuts, and a splash of balsamic vinaigrette.

Another easy way to consume heaps of veggies is to drink them in smoothies and juices. My go-to smoothie recipe is two-to-three overflowing handfuls of spinach, one-to-two cups of frozen or fresh fruit, a few baby carrots, a cup of unsweetened almond milk, a spoonful of coconut oil, half an avocado, and sprinkles of protein powder, chia seeds, and/or flax seeds. Lots of fat and protein to satiate!

Soups are another simple way to eat your veggies. My favorite is a veggie cassoulet filled with beans, carrots, potatoes, onion, vegetable bouillon, and a few savory rosemary sprigs. Yummy served hot or cold.

More of a snacker? Pack a bag of crunchy baby carrots to help offset a tempting afternoon jaunt to the vending machine. Try celery dipped in sugar-free peanut butter for a crunchy protein kick. Slice avocado and sprinkle it with Montreal steak seasoning (my favorite spice). Make kale chips. Nosh on sweet potato hummus with whole wheat pita bread.

Strive to create a colorful plate. It's encouraged that we have an assortment of colors every day—blue and purple (eggplant, cabbage), red (radishes, tomatoes), green (leafy greens, broccoli), white (cauliflower, onions), yellow (corn, butternut squash), orange (sweet potatoes, carrots). Next time you sit down to savor a meal, notice the colors in front of you.

Is your meal processed or from a box? No judgment, just notice. From there you can make simple, small, colorful, whole food changes.

This week, spice up your plate with a few cancer-fighting, immune-boosting vibrant veggies. Spare the animals, conserve the environment, and honor your health. A true win-win!

Week 26: Write

The blank page beckons with the opportunity to unleash emotions, memories, fantasies, and dreams.

Writing is a blend of vulnerability and empowerment. Hemingway said, "There is nothing to writing. All you do is sit down at a typewriter and bleed." Yep, full-fledged vulnerability.

I grew up listening to the dings and taps of my father's Underwood typewriter as he wrote into the wee hours. The instrument provided the chance to create and share. I was smitten.

For years, my writing was mainly an emotional outlet to capture struggles and explore relationships in a lined spiral-bound journal. Then I began writing for my yoga studio—newsletters, agreements, marketing materials. Shortly thereafter I found my way to blogging, writing books, studying writing, and occasionally teaching about the writing practice.

My journey continues to evolve the more I learn and explore. It's a practice ripe with possibility. And the best part? There's no one way to do it. Love notes, snail mail, memos, journal writing, essays, articles, op-eds, books: the options are limitless.

Yet to write takes time, effort, and the desire to bleed . . . at least a little.

Writing has been shown to speed up emotional and physical healing, help change our perspective, and leads to long-term improvements in mood, stress levels, and depressive symptoms. So it looks like it may be worth the bleeding.

What do you feel bubbling up inside? Does the thought of a blinking cursor or a blank sheet of paper make you queasy? Is there a book idea swirling around in your mind?

Begin with pen and paper or a Word document titled "Writing." Simple. Write what's on your mind. Write what's keeping you up at night. Write about the day your life changed. Write about your scar. Write about your relationship. Write the back cover copy for your memoir. Write your eulogy.

Make writing a priority this week. Capture a few minutes during your lunch hour to describe the setting you're in. Jot your dreams. Record your day with sensory details. Share what you're feeling. Translate what's in your head onto paper and observe what unfolds. Judgment is not invited to the practice.

Bleed a little and let magic happen.

Week 27: Pen Month's Dreams

Welcome to the second half of the year. Connection to your New Year's resolutions may feel like a distant memory or different era, as if penned by someone else. I wanted to do *what*?!

Staying connected to larger aspirations is why I encourage writing out your dreams for the month. Then the bigger picture won't get lost with the laundry, bills, workouts, and day job.

Sit down and reflect on this month's dreams. Assess how you're doing in pursuit of your bigger goals. This helps avoid the "rinse and repeat" syndrome—get up, go to work, watch TV, go to bed.

Make it an Artist's Date. Grab your *Daybook*, crafting supplies (washi tape is a must!), and a Sharpie.

Begin by reviewing the previous month and note what you accomplished. Day at the lake. Check. Time with family. Check. Complete big project at work. Check. Daily meditation. Oops.

Carry over any of the oops— you know, the ones with the best of intentions, which didn't quite come to fruition. Confession: About a quarter of my monthly dreams fit this category.

Next, add flair to your *Daybook*. Don't worry, if you don't have a *Daybook*, you can do this in any planner or on a plain sheet of white paper.

After the flair has been added, pen the big happenings on your radar: workshops, meetings, retreats, projects, classes, travel, and special dates such as birthdays or anniversaries.

Then ponder those bigger annual dreams (yep, the ones from the new year) and add an aligned action step into this month's spread. For example, if a dream this year was to complete a book proposal, add "write chapter summaries" to your month's dreams.

Ponder the personal goals you'd like to make a priority this month and add them with a pretty pink marker. Consider "weekly date nights," "take four yoga classes," or "finish reading memoir." Self-care deserves the same level of attention as projects on deadline.

Make this a sensory-filled ritual. Set aside 30 minutes this week, light a candle, and surround yourself with your favorite art supplies. Let your inner artist play.

Acknowledge last month's efforts and get excited about this brand new one beckoning you to make the most of it. You deserve it. And so do your dreams.

Week 28: P.M. Routine

Picture yourself curled up with a journal, taking a few moments to exhale after a productive day. Ah, an evening routine.

Your P.M. routine is the bookend to your A.M. routine (week 17). This time ties a bow around your day and sets the tone for what's to come tomorrow.

For many, it's decompression time to unwind, restore, and replenish. Ideally with a cuppa tea and furry friend nearby.

How do you spend your day's finale?

Do you flop on the couch, kick up your heels, and surf the Internet? Make a meal, pull out a book, and connect with loved ones? Channel surf looking for entertainment while eating processed food mindlessly? At times, guilty as charged.

At bedtime, are you on the computer going down rabbit holes, answering emails, or savoring a soak in the tub?

No judgment, just observe your pattern. Is it serving you? Does it set you up for success or leave you drained?

The moments before we close our eyes are time to prepare our bodies (and minds) for the following day. Create an evening routine that works for you and your lifestyle.

Consider an electronic shutdown time for computers, TVs, and phones. This allows your mind to unwind without external stimulation. Instead of technology, connect to your breath or try a few restorative yoga poses. To avoid random text messages and phone calls, set your smartphone to Do Not Disturb. For me, that's 10 p.m. – 8 a.m.

Write in your journal. Soak in the tub. List gratitude and lessons learned from your day. Connect with loved ones—fur babies and humans. Prep for the next day by choosing your outfit, packing lunch, and setting out any workout gear. Avoid alcohol or caffeine (yes, that means chocolate) within a few hours of bedtime.

Clear clutter and review your next day's priorities. Set your alarm to allow seven to nine hours of sleep. Create a setting conducive to relaxation. Lower the thermostat to keep your body cool. Spritz your linens with lavender spray. Dab lavender oil on your temples. Insert earplugs and don your eye pillow.

This wind-down process can be accomplished in five minutes, or if you have the luxury, 60. This week, clarify how you want to close the day so it complements your morning routine in a healthy, holistic way.

The few hours you have post-work/pre-sleep may vaporize if a routine isn't set. Plan ahead to make your evenings intentional. Get the sleep you need. Use your personal time to ground, reflect, and gear up for the next day's adventures. Nighty-night and happy slumbering.

Week 29: Mindful Eating

Take a raisin in your hand. Observe its texture. Smell its fragrance. Squeeze it by your ear and notice any sounds. Put it on your tongue and move it around your mouth with full awareness of the sensations.

Take one bite into the raisin and notice a burst of flavor. Slowly chew it into tiny pieces until there is nothing left. Observe how much time this takes. Visit kimberlywilson.com/52weeks for a raisin meditation mp3.

The raisin meditation is one of the first practices in an 8-week Mindfulness-Based Stress Reduction (MBSR) course and it never ceases to amaze me. Paying attention to such a small object is a strong reminder to slow down and savor.

Truth be told, most of my meals are eaten at a brisk pace navigating projects, clients, and meetings. Savoring texture, smell, sound, and taste are ongoing intentions.

However, getting the object of desire into my belly is typically the focus. And unfortunately, sometimes a complete meal is gone before I've even truly tasted what was consumed. All of a sudden, it's finished!

During a MBSR teacher training, we spent many meals in silence and it served as a great wake-up call to savor versus shovel.

Although I continued to semi-shovel my steel-cut oats with fresh berries, I did so with awareness and the intention to set down my fork between every few bites.

Throughout the day, I held a cuppa jasmine tea in my hands. Felt the warmth, smelled the fragrance, tasted the floral essence, and noticed the liquid slide down my throat. Mindfulness can also be practiced with our beverages (See Week 24: Sip Tea).

At the end of the training we created mindfulness action plans and one participant was determined to eat a few meals each week without doing anything else at the same time—no reading, talking, Internet, TV, or any other distraction.

This week, take time to savor your food and drinks. Eat in silence *sans* distractions. Notice when you're hungry and full. Observe what you're eating. Connect with your senses—colors, sounds, flavors, temperatures, textures, and tastes. Notice how you feel after eating.

Try a meal in silence solo, without doing anything else. Encourage your family, friend, or partner to join you in slowly eating in silence for the first few minutes. Take the first sips of your favorite libation with full attention.

Week 30: Practice Acceptance

When the vet tech returned to let us know that they weren't going to need a spinal tap for Louis, I knew. They'd found something during the MRI that explained the sneezing and seizure, and it wasn't good.

Minutes passed, feeling like days, before the doctor came out to give us the news. There was a large mass in the nasal cavity that had grown into his brain. It was inoperable. My body went numb, head dropped, and tears welled.

Louis had been our baby since he was eight weeks old. We fed him organic grain-free food, rushed him to the vet if anything seemed off (e.g. sprained toe), and tended to his every wish. We expected to have him five more years. I mean, 12 to 15 years is the average life span of a pug and he was in tip-top shape.

Or so we thought.

Everything changed that brisk January day and collapsed when we said goodbye a few months later. The unconditional love of a pet is incomparable and he was a special case. I may have been known to refer him as "the love of my life."

When Tim and I began the adoption process weeks after losing Louis, I said to a colleague, "If I don't get a dog soon, I may die." Okay, slightly Scarlett O'Hara, but also telling of how integrated and sacred his presence was in my life.

Once we signed the paperwork to adopt our new rescue, Mookie (photo below), I felt joy that I hadn't experienced since before Louis' diagnosis. It was palpable. I was lighter and had an outlet for an outpouring of love.

I recently began reading *Writing to Heal the Soul: Transforming Grief and Loss Through Writing* and the author begins by unpacking expectations. How was it supposed to be? What did you expect? What was the change of plans?

This is an interesting exercise for so many of our losses—jobs, friendships, love, family, health, children, pets, etc.

The author notes, "A large part of coming to terms with loss is dealing with our expectations of what 'should have been.' Until we articulate those expectations, we cannot move beyond them. We are stuck in the 'Why me?' litany."

For me, I thought if we fed him the right food, kept him fit and trim (not easy for a pug), showered him with love, and took him in for all his vaccinations and vet needs, we'd have him until age 15. This expectation shaped my mindset and heightened the shock of a brain cancer diagnosis.

It's not that we shouldn't have had these high hopes for our boy, but rather a reminder to acknowledge how little control we have. What we *do* have control over is our response to disappointment, tragedy, and loss.

Viktor Frankl wrote in *Man's Search for Meaning*, "Everything can be taken from a man but one thing: the last of human freedoms—to choose one's attitude in any given set of circumstances, to choose one's way."

And sometimes one's way is to accept, rather than fight, what's transpired.

While I miss Louis terribly, I choose to celebrate our 10.5 years together. Although our new boy Mookie will never replace him, he offered a beautiful bond that has been desperately missed. Again, acceptance.

Is there a situation in your life that hasn't worked out as you'd expected? You may be asking yourself "which one?!" as life can be full of them! What would acceptance look like in one of these situations?

Remember, acceptance doesn't lessen the pain, rather it curbs the continual striving for things to be different than they are. What requests acceptance in your life?

Week 31: Embrace Minimalism

Capsule dressing. Tiny houses. Mono-tasking. Simplicity. Mindfulness. Digital detoxes. A.M. and P.M. rituals. Essentialism. Slowing down. Decluttering. Intentional screen time. Inventory of possessions. Downsizing. Less stress. No debt.

You may wonder, what do these possibly have in common? They are minimalism concepts!

During my early commuting days, I'd often have a big fat book on simplicity tucked into my tote. Oh the irony, from *Simple Abundance* to *The Simple Living Guide*—these books were 400–500+ pages!

Since my first introductions to simple living in the late 90s, an entire genre of bloggers, books, and consultants have emerged touting minimalism.

The Internet is filled with wonderful minimalist lifestyle resources: Into-Mind, The Minimalists, Be More With Less, Zen Habits, and Rowdy Kittens (*Tranquility du Jour* podcasts #207, #253, #259) to name a few. But what *exactly* is it?

According to *Becoming Minimalist*, minimalism is "The intentional promotion of the things we most value and the removal of everything that distracts us from it." Seems simple and noble, right? Yet not necessarily easy.

Since reading and rereading Francine Jay's *The Joy of Less, A Minimalist Living Guide*, I've been much more cognizant of purchasing habits. Rather than shopping or thrifting for fun, I ask myself if I *really* need it before pulling out my credit card. The end of random drop-ins to Target or similar discount stores has left me with more time, money, and space for other things—mainly experiences.

I've also been on a mission to own less stuff. As someone drawn to vintage items, home accessories (hello white pug bookends and pink pig watering can), and sparkly things, this has taken a conscious shift. Regular purges of books help offset my book-buying tendencies. Cleaning closets and donating outworn or unused shoes and clothes is a seasonal event.

In addition, using my tea and stationery stashes *before* purchasing new ones has also helped me pare down.

Think about where you spend your time and money. Is it serving you?

While I may struggle with book-buying, your drug of choice may be TV time or shoe shopping.

Consider for a moment: if you cut that activity in half, what would you gain? More time? Less debt? More space?

This week, try one of these tiny steps toward minimalism. Avoid buying anything unnecessary. Declutter. Mix and match the same clothing items all week. Eat similar things (e.g., make a big batch of steel-cut oats and enjoy it each morning).

Donate anything unworn in the past six months. Unsubscribe from magazines, emails, blogs, and podcasts that no longer serve you. Turn off the TV. Mono-task. Slow your pace. Stop overcommitting. Meditate.

May you find time and space for what matters most.

Week 32: Drink Your Greens

Despite being veg for nearly two decades, I'll often reach for anything but veggies when given a choice.

Sprinkled glazed donut? Okay! Pizza? Absolutely! Fruit? Give it to me!

But greens, well, not on my must-have list with the exception of a big arugula or spinach salad with perfectly tangy lemon dressing.

When introduced to the world of green smoothies in 2010 and green juices shortly thereafter, my veggie consumption skyrocketed.

To make these vitamin-infused babies, I invested in a refurbished Vitamix (a basic blender works, too) and then a Breville Juice Fountain Compact.

Now you can find pre-packaged green drinks at many grocery stores, and even gas stations! My yoga studio carries a few small-batched creations for the yogi needing a boost on-the-go. The great news is they're everywhere!

The benefits touted are many—flooding your system with vitamins and nutrients, being quicker to consume than chewing a salad, increasing energy, improving digestion, reducing inflammation, stabilizing blood sugar, enhancing mental clarity (bye bye white flour and sugar which are said to cloud the mind), improving immunity. I mean, wow, right?

So what's the difference between juicing juices and blending smoothies? Juicing separates juice from the fiber and blending blends all the ingredients together. Some prefer one over the other. For me, it depends on mood, creativity (e.g. which ingredients are on hand), and time (juicing tends to take longer).

Blending is a simple starting point for drinking greens and it's best to shoot for three veggies to each fruit. Juicing allows you to get more veggies (AND nutrients) inside since the fiber is removed.

You may be saying, "I know, I know it's good for me, but where do I begin?" Picture me taking your hand and leading you into my tiny kitchen, taking you through the steps below, and sending you off with a belly full of greens, glowing skin, and a happy heart. You're not alone.

This week, play with one of the recipes above or a few of the many online. Mix and match your favorite fruits and veggies with a powerhouse such as chia, hemp, or flaxseed and coconut oil. Spice it up with a bit of ginger or turmeric. Add good creamy fat with avocado or coconut oil.

GREEN JUICE* RECIPE:

1 green apple
4 stalks celery
1 cucumber
4 handfuls spinach
6 kale leaves
1/2 peeled lemon
1 piece fresh ginger

* Don't have a juicer? Don't despair, you can still make juice with a blender. Google for tips on how to do so.

GREEN SMOOTHIE RECIPE:

2 handfuls spinach
1 tablespoon chia seeds**
1 cup almond milk or water
1/2 avocado**
1 tablespoon coconut oil**
1 apple--unpeeled, cored, and chopped
1/2 lemon--peeled and chopped

** These offer good fats to help you feel full along with heaps of nutrients!

Week 33: Walk

Lift, place, shift. This is the basic instruction for walking meditation. Over and over again, without a destination.

Simple, often on autopilot, yet overflowing with benefits, walking is en vogue.

Great minds such as Steve Jobs, Henry David Thoreau, and Virginia Woolf used walking to think better, gain energy, and conduct meetings.

I mean, they're pretty solid endorsements, right?

Goodness, there's even a TED Talk touting the benefits in which the speaker, Nilofer Merchant, claims that sitting is the new smoking. She estimates that we're sitting approximately 10 hours a day and this takes a toll on our energy, state of mind, and physical health.

A friend of mine began getting off the Metro a few stops before her usual and lost 100 pounds from her daily 90-minute walking commute!

Walking proponent Geoff Nicholson, author of *The Lost Art of Walking*, recommends partaking in this beneficial activity *sans* phone, music, podcasts, or audiobooks. Yep, just the pure act of one foot in front of the other.

The French have a word for this activity—*flâneur*—to stroll leisurely without a destination in mind. When's the last time you allowed yourself this pleasure?

In a 2014 Stanford University study, walking increased participants' creativity by 81%. Thoreau wrote in his journal that when his legs move, thoughts begin to flow.

Have a problem to solve or a brainstorming meeting to attend? Feeling sluggish mid-day? Put on comfy shoes and hit the pavement for fresh air, a change of scenery, and a shift away from the screen.

Walking is said to lift the spirits, strengthen memory, and decrease the risk of some cancers. 30 minutes per day is recommended. Sound impossible? Try 15 in the morning and 15 in the evening. Weave it into your daily routine this week.

Week 34: Signature Style

Red lips. Leopard-print scarf. Hasbeen clogs. Black head to toe. Plastic black rose ring. Faux pearl earrings. Nude-colored mani. Gold pleather tote.

Washi tape. Handwritten thank-you notes. Colored pens. Overuse of words like "hot mess," "sweet pea," and "dude."

Pink walls. Twinkle lights. Scented candles. Black furry creatures. Fresh flowers. Chandeliers.

Black matte frame, pink details, white wall wheels.

The above descriptions highlight my chosen signature style in dress, communication, home, and transportation. This photo showcases my Farm Sanctuary style and, yes, I was the only one in a skirt and polka-dot trimmed rain boots playing with pigs.

How would you describe your signature style?

Signature style is the way you present yourself to the world. It's how you share what you love and feel through actions and words.

Below are a few iconic styles:

COCO CHANEL: LBD (little black dress), layers of pearls, tweed blazer.

BETSEY JOHNSON: does the splits on stage during her runway shows, wears tutus, bright colors, and has platinum blond hair.

AUDREY HEPBURN: ballet flats, cropped pants, black crew neck sweater, striped shirt.

SHABBY CHIC: a flea market style of pastels, slipcovers, chandeliers, overstuffed chairs, and distressed furniture.

Consider Anthropologie versus Chicos, Motel 6 versus The Ritz, or your local gym versus a favorite yoga studio—each has a unique trademark, its very own signature style.

Signature style evolves.

13 years ago I loved dressing in pink and green. 20 years ago I could be found in preppy Black Watch plaid paired with holey Levis. Now I only don jeans *sans* holes on rare occasions.

I used to decorate with dark wood, hunter green, ivy, pansies, and *papier-mâché* fruit. Now I choose peonies, pink, chandeliers, and damask.

Way back when, I only sent quirky Mary Engelbreit or sentimental Flavia cards to family and friends. Now I prefer colorful notecards from paper stores, Etsy, or big box dollar bins.

Who knows how this will evolve over the next few decades. The beauty of it is we don't have to know, we can let our style unfold as our taste changes, trends shift, and we continue to come more and more into our own.

You've seen *Advanced Style* and *Iris*, right?

How would someone describe your signature style? How do *you* describe it? How do you want to present yourself? Do you feel comfortable in your own skin?

If not, what changes would you like to make? If so, how has it evolved and how would you like it to continue to do so? You are one of a kind and are invited to showcase it every single day. Play with your signature style expression this week.

Week 35: Journal

Thoughts and emotions swirl like an internal storm.

It's early, the house is still sleeping and I'm sitting at my desk surrounded by writing supplies, but paralyzed by where to begin.

I reach for my notebook and pen, sink into the plush damask chair, and release this inner cacophony onto the page.

This therapeutic process is called journaling.

Studies show that it helps stimulate creativity, brings mindfulness to a wandering mind, process post-traumatic stress disorder, increase sleep, decrease stress and anxiety, and even decrease cancer symptoms.

I've been an avid pen-to-paper gal since grade school, when I'd observe my Gramma spending her evening toiling away in a notebook, detailing her day. So I, too, created a practice to highlight my latest grade school crush or BFF.

Over the years, I began to use my journal for processing bigger decisions in life like, "should I stay or should I go?" This allowed me to leave places, positions, and relationships I'd outgrown.

As a therapist, I often encourage clients to jot down emotions, thoughts, and physical sensations between our sessions. To note what triggered a reaction and to be a curious observer of their own lives. It's powerful stuff and helps us see others and ourselves more clearly.

Similar to any practice you begin—writing, yoga, cooking—it's all about exercising the muscle regularly and creating a habit.

Maybe you start with a gratitude journal, keep it by your bedside, and list one thing you're grateful for before going to sleep. Or you invest in a Moleskine and tote it with you everywhere you go. Or you keep a basic spiral-bound Mead notebook on your desk to pull out as needed.

The point of the practice is to, well, make it a regular practice.

My favorite go-to prompt when I'm feeling stuck or find myself staring at a blank page longer than I'd like is, "How am I feeling right now?" I tap into it from all angles—mental, physical, spiritual, emotional.

This week, set aside at least ten minutes to sit with your thoughts and note what comes up. Consider writing about the end of summer (or winter for those in the Southern Hemisphere), dreams for next season, a dilemma you're struggling with, or lists such as "my favorite things."

Grab paper and pen and watch what unfolds.

Week 36: Oil Up

Sitting at my desk overlooking the garden, I'm coated in a variety of oils.

After bathing, I douse my body in sweet almond oil and my face in some assortment of argan oil, rosehip oil, jojoba oil, apricot oil, and essential oils, preferably jasmine.

Or if I'm in a hurry, I stick with straight argan oil before dashing out the door.

Face and body oils have become quite popular over the past few years and I've jumped on the bandwagon, courtesy of having been gifted a few.

For years, I loved lathering myself in scented body lotions such as Pineapple Mango Mint (or other random concoctions). Then a fellow yogi mentioned how the skin was our largest organ (yep, all 8 pounds and 22 square feet of it) and so she preferred natural oils to chemicals.

This made perfect sense and began my love affair with oils. I found silky soft skin in a large bottle of sweet almond oil.

Sweet almond oil is a reasonably priced option with skin, hair, and health benefits, such as soothing stressed muscles, helping ease skin conditions, moisturizing, reducing fine lines, and nourishing processed hair. It absorbs quickly and has no scent. A great starter and staple to have on hand.

Next I graduated to argan oil after reading about it as the multitasker oil. It's touted as a miracle oil for hair, skin, nails, lips, dry feet, stretch marks, acne, aging skin, and more.

Recently I even made my own face oil blend using rosehip oil, jojoba oil, sweet almond oil, and sunflower oil topped with drops of rose, jasmine, and sandalwood essential oils. Clearly I'm a convert.

Linda Rodin is my example of aging gracefully. This woman exudes style—silver hair, pink lips, mascara, funky glasses. Her face oil blend is my indulgence and when I dab a drop or two onto my face, it's pure luxury. Shortly after beginning to use it, a few friends commented on how great my skin looked, so I knew I'd found a gem.

Even the sister science of yoga, Ayurveda, encourages a daily *Abyanga* practice—a 15–20-minute head-to-toe self-massage with warm oils *before* bathing. It's touted as a stress reduction and detox therapy that helps us connect with and love our bodies.

There are many oils to choose from and numerous uses for the oils. This week, dabble with sweet almond oil (unless you have a nut allergy) or rosehip oil. Look for certified organic and cold-pressed, if available. Begin with your body, and as you get braver, add to your face, hair, and nails regimen. Adorn your skin with loving layers, one stroke at a time.

Week 37: Soak in the Tub

After a full day shuffling from clients to meetings to teaching, nothing heals like a soak in the tub. It's a full body-and-soul balm.

Immersing in water provides mental, physical, and spiritual benefits. When my body aches, my mind is tired, or my heart feels heavy, to the bath I go. And, honestly, many moments in between.

If it's frigid outside, the only way to warm my bones is a hot bath. As temperatures drop in the city, a nightly soak will become my norm. Bring it on, fall!

Many, many years ago (4500 B.C.) baths were touted as a cure for mental illness. While we no longer give bathing that degree of power, I have found that water *does* provide healing—it soothes, comforts, and nurtures. According to Isak Dinesen, "The cure for anything is salt water. Sweat, tears, or the sea."

To make your bath a sensory-filled experience, enhance it with spa-like touches. Light candles. Dim lights (helps hide the pet hair, too). Turn on relaxing tunes. Have a cool libation within reach.

Run hot water to your liking—I tend to run it on the hot side so that as it cools, I'm still cozy warm. Add bath oil (love me some sweet almond oil), essential oils, bath salts, or bath tea.

Close your eyes. Let yourself go. Stay at least 20 minutes. Towel off and massage with a moisturizing body oil. Slip into a fluffy robe and slippers to read before bed or enjoy your breakfast before launching into the day.

If a bath isn't an option, consider another form of body self-care where you can let go and relax. Maybe it's a steam at the gym or a long shower at home. Give yourself a weekly—ideally, daily—dose of watery relaxation.

Benefits include relieving muscle aches, calming the mind, reducing cramps, aiding sleep, fighting cold symptoms (hello, steam), increasing circulation (hello, sweat), detoxifying, and more. I deem these fairly strong benefits for 20 minutes of sitting in warm water!

A soak resembles a massage. Although it's not the same as having my muscles manipulated, it's cheaper, readily available *sans* appointment, and offers me a comparable state of deep relaxation.

This week, find 30 minutes in your schedule to set up, savor, and transition from a 20-minute soak. Enveloped in warm water, observe your mind still and your body melt.

Week 38: Entertain

Light candles. Display flowers. Create a libation station of wine, tea, and water with mint sprigs. Set out finger-friendly *hors d'oeuvres* on silver platters with doilies. Dim the lights. Remove pet hair and relocate kids' toys.

This is my basic day-of-entertaining checklist and what runs through my head continually before greeting the first guest.

Hosting an intimate dinner for two or a cocktail party for 20 doesn't have to be a grand feat. Make the event a stress-free endeavor with mindful planning.

Below are 8 steps for ease-filled entertaining:

1. **WEEKS OR MONTHS OUT** (depending on your *soirée* size): Choose theme, date, time.

2. **SEND INVITATIONS AND COLLECT RSVPS.** Expect 30% not to respond and 15% of those who do not to show.

3. **WEEKS OR DAYS OUT:** Accumulate dry goods such as candles, candied nuts, cloth napkins, guest gifts, or any additional glasses or dishware you may need. Thrift stores offer unique, one-of-a-kind pieces at a great price.

4. **DAY OF:** Create food, gather flowers, clean the house (focus on the loo), tie bows around stemware (seriously, it's my thing), and decorate (try twinkle lights, bunting, streamers, chalkboard signs or seasonal items such as pumpkins, fall leaves, and pine cones).

5. **A FEW HOURS BEFORE:** Set a festive table and bar, design a centerpiece with votives and flowers, light candles, pack goody bags, and turn on mood music. Prep *hors d'oeuvres* such as mini quiches, grilled tofu skewers, avocado crostinis, and bruschetta. Display and identify them with name cards. Make the food an artistic presentation with sprigs of rosemary, pomegranate seeds, or flowers. Try frozen *hors d'oeuvres* from your local grocery store served as tapas, followed by delicate macarons from a French bakery. Your creativity may lie in the decor and hostessing, rather than the food itself. It definitely does for me!

6. **SLIP INTO SOMETHING COMFORTABLE** that allows you to move, feels good on your skin, and is a signature piece. No sense in having your outfit be a source of stress on your big day.

7. **WELCOME GUESTS,** introduce them to each other, offer beverages, take coats and bags, and let your inner Martha Stewart shine.

8. **RELAX INTO THE EXPERIENCE.** Guests pick up on anxiety or discomfort and follow suit. Have fun, lighten expectations, and challenge yourself to go with the flow.

When hosting, you don't have to make everything from scratch. Entertaining can be a creative endeavor even without going to culinary school. Your only "recipe" may be adding heirloom tomatoes, mandarin oranges, green apple slices, and candied pecans to a bowl of arugula.

Entertaining helps facilitate a deep clean and removal of paper piles that grow without regular curation. This is an added bonus and may be motivation enough to schedule a *fête*.

This week, host an impromptu tea party with a friend, schedule a cocktail party in celebration of fall, or make one of your regular family meals a festive experience.

Week 39: Review Budget

Spend less than you make. While this is the basic premise of budgeting, it gets more complex.

For those of us who still love and use paper, it's a simple balance sheet for regular review.

To create a budget, begin by listing your income sources such as paychecks, freelance work, and residual income.

Next, list your various expenses, starting with fixed costs such as rent/mortgage, car payments, insurance, Internet, yoga membership, and student loans.

Then add in the additional ones that may vary slightly each month, such as entertainment, electricity, dining out, gifts, donations, groceries, clothing, and pet and/or child care.

If you're not clear on where the money goes each month, track everything you spend—from the soy chai latte to the I-forgot-my-lunch meal out. Writing down everything you buy for a few months offers great insight into your outflow.

The goal, of course, is to have money left over after the monthly reconciliation of income and expenses. This extra can be moved into savings or a rainy day fund to help cover unexpected incidents (like your cat eating rubber bands and having them surgically removed). True story.

Experts encourage us to have six months in reserve in case of emergency or those unpredictable events.

One way to facilitate this is to have a percentage pulled out of your paycheck and put into savings and/or investments before it hits your bank account. Handy for ensuring self-control. Also handy for self-control is the Stretching Your Dollar piece on p. 120 of my first book, *Hip Tranquil Chick*. For example, bake cookies or make soap versus buying a gift.

I've been using mint.com for a few years and receive a weekly notification straight to my inbox on my budget. It's quite handy, except when receiving a shaming email noting "unusual spending on shoes." I blame the Swedish Hasbeens sale for that one.

This week, set up a budget to note your financial habits. Explore what's working and what needs tweaking. It's never too late to begin this process and get your financial life in order.

Visit kimberlywilson.com/52weeks for a downloadable budget worksheet.

Week 40: Volunteer

After filling my plate with formerly frozen pieces of cut fruit and mini pastries, I took my seat in a windowless conference room at Washington Hospice. I was honoring the anniversary of my Gramma's death by going through a two-day volunteer training to work with people during their final days of life.

Since then I've been showing up regularly for three-hour shifts to sit with patients, fetch them or their family members anything they need, and offer support to patients and nursing staff.

Recently I sat outside with a patient in the final stages of lung cancer while he switched between smoking a cigarette and puffing on his inhaler. We discussed the weather, his career as a plumber in D.C., and our mutual passion for chewy candy.

My introduction to volunteering began by dressing up in tutus in grade school dance class and performing for nursing home patients.

Over the years my volunteer hat has included petting and feeding pigs at sanctuaries, holiday caroling, leading teens through a tranquility-based curriculum, correcting envelope misprints for a political campaign, serving Thanksgiving meals at a senior center, teaching charity yoga at Tranquil Space, taking homeless women to a sewing lounge to learn a new trade, hosting fundraisers, and offering chair yoga to seniors at an assisted living center.

I share this to show how the process of giving back is as varied as the volunteers themselves. According to the Bureau of Labor Statistics, 62.8 million Americans volunteered in 2014 with a median of 50 hours—averaging out to approximately one hour/week. The website Idealist lists four steps to finding or creating the right volunteer opportunity: Identify potential partner organizations, determine fit, get to know the organization and opportunity, make a decision.

This week, consider your role as a volunteer. Do you have a spot that feels right? Is there an organization you'd like to connect with on a deeper level? Are you aware of the many ways in which you already donate your time, money, and energy? Honor your efforts and keep exploring ways to make a difference. It starts from within and has a ripple effect on your family, community, and the world. No biggie!

Week 41: Create

Ah, the elusive practice of creating. Until early adulthood I believed that only a few chosen ones were blessed with the creative gene. That had clearly passed me by. Art class was as awkward for me as gym class and I couldn't help but notice that my painted birds, rainbows, or landscapes never looked like the others'.

It simply wasn't my gift. It was little Johnny's or Susie's, but not mine.

Upon reading Julia Cameron's *The Artist's Way*, my impression of creativity took a turn from feeling passed over by the art fairy to believing that everything we do can be a chance to create. Our daily routine offers numerous opportunities to create. We get up in the morning and choose something to wear. We may exercise, make breakfast, read, or write. Then we may head to a day job where we have the opportunity to create—teach, write, work with clients, collaborate with colleagues, manage projects. We may head home to exercise (if it didn't make it into the morning), meet with friends, make dinner, or read.

All of these daily activities can be creative expressions of who we are and how we see the world.

Tuck a love note into your partner's bag or child's lunchbox. Try a new recipe. Sprinkle flax seed on your steel cut oats. Add ginger to your green juice. Write with a gold pen. Participate in a book club. Listen to motivating music or a podcast on your way to work. Light a candle. Add fresh flowers to your desk.

Bake treats for your office. Make your Halloween costume from no-longer-worn items in your closet (flapper is always fun). Join an improv troupe. Start a writing group. Get a creativity accountability buddy. Plant a garden (windowsill herb box counts). Start a family or date night ritual. Take up handicrafts such as embroidery, knitting, crochet, or cross-stitch.

Paint your nails fire engine red. Read a different genre. Send snail mail with a treat tucked inside. Write a book proposal. Start a blog. Launch a podcast. Accessorize. Pull out a paintbrush and play in your art journal. Take a dance class. Sign up for piano lessons.

Remember, it's never too late. Next year you'll be one year older either way; so why not dabble in creative practices that interest you?

In *Big Magic*, Elizabeth Gilbert reminds us that creativity is "your birthright as a human being," that "even if you grew up watching cartoons in a sugar stupor from dawn to dusk, creativity still lurks within you," and that "you are not required to save the world with your creativity."

This week, create something. Anything. How was the process? What surprised you? What scared you? What do you want to create next?

Week 42: Productivity

Wondering how to conquer your never-ending to-do list or to avoid the exhaustion that comes with putting out fire after fire?

When asked how I juggle various projects, I give full credit to writing everything down—getting it out of my head and onto paper. Yes, *everything*. With a gold pen.

I carry my *Daybook*, an ideas book, and occasionally a journal. In order to be productive, I must stay mindful and organized.

My most helpful tool is clarifying weekly, and sometimes daily, M.I.T.s (Most Important Tasks). Noting what must be accomplished that day/week helps put the rest of the to-dos in perspective.

Yes, laundry needs to be done, but not before the document on deadline is reviewed.

Also, break projects into smaller tasks, so instead of "launch fall collection," try "choose colors and order lab dips." This lessens overwhelm and breaks big chunks into bite-sized pieces.

To avoid switching hats multiple times throughout the day, set times for checking email, writing, working on projects, handling home, exercise, relaxation, and family. That way you can be fully present with the person or task in front of you.

For example, I don my therapist hat three days a week, writer hat on Monday (and ideally other days in between), podcast interviewer hat on Friday, workshop facilitator hat on the weekend, mindfulness teacher hat on Monday, and so on.

Task-switching among various hats can thwart my ability to stay focused and in the zone. One study found that recovering from interruption typically takes 23 minutes and 15 seconds to return to the original task. Wow!

Setting social media and email (especially those pesky notifications) aside for big chunks also helps to mono-task versus multi-task, which studies show makes us dumber (See Week 6: Single-Task).

Productivity needs rest. One of the biggest lessons I've learned during the past 16 years of entrepreneurship is to step away from the computer, breathe, and say "yes!" to date requests with girlfriends or Tim, even if I have more to-dos (there always are). There are few things that a hot bath and good sleep can't fix (or at least offer a fresh perspective on).

This week, consider your daily level of productivity. Where can you lighten expectations, clarify your M.I.T.s, and don fewer hats? Insert doses of rest, play, whole foods, and exercise. Watch your productivity soar.

Week 43: Body Scan

It's mid-afternoon on a sunny June day with a slight breeze and sounds of singing birds. I'm lying on the floor looking up at the exposed wooden beams in a large room at Omega—a spiritual retreat center in upstate New York.

Jon Kabat-Zinn is walking 200 therapists through a 45-minute body scan as I struggle to keep my eyes open. His voice is soothing and has a tendency to lull me to sleep.

I make it through from the toes to the hips and wake up while he's referencing the ears. Gasp, I've missed most of the body scan! And, truth be told, this continued the rest of the week.

A body scan is considered a deep investigation into the moment-to-moment experiences of the body. It's an important part of the 8-week Mindfulness-Based Stress Reduction course created by Jon in 1979 and now taught globally. The practice encourages a shift from our busy thinking mind to all the parts of the body.

The practice begins at the toes and travels all the way up to the top of the head to bring awareness to the body. To say "hello" with a sense of loving-kindness and to notice any stress, tension, or tightness it may be holding.

Martha Graham noted that "the body says what words cannot," and a body scan gives us the opportunity to listen. The body communicates through physical sensations, thoughts, and emotions—and this is referred to as the "triangle of awareness."

Physical sensations can be a key to our emotional state. Notice what happens in the body when you run into a challenging colleague, get stuck in traffic, or receive an upsetting email. The body reacts.

Although the practice is typically done lying down, try it during your next meeting, unnecessary conference call, or in conflict with your significant other.

Bring awareness to the feeling of your toes in your shoes and move up the legs to the hips, belly and back, fingers, arms, shoulders, chest, and head.

This week, try a body scan. There's an 11-minute mp3 at kimberlywilson.com/52weeks and many more available online.

Week 44: Self-Care

It's 9 p.m. when I walk through the door. I greet my loved ones, open the refrigerator and reach for a cold-pressed green juice, pour crystallized lemon into my monogrammed mug, top it with boiling water, and then head to the bath for a long soak. This is an ideal evening of good self-care.

An example of the opposite is coming home after a long day and heading straight to my desk, popping open my laptop and continuing to work on additional projects—clothing line, studio, writing and the ultimate drain, email.

When my clients express frustration with emotional regulation and reactivity, the first thing I ask is about their self-care. Often I'll hear a sigh and notice a shift in their posture.

Yes, sleep has been inadequate lately. Yes, they've been eating poorly. Yes, their yoga practice has stopped. Yes, there's overwhelm with little relief in sight.

And, yes, self-care has been placed on the back burner, they confess. Who has time for that? Sound or feel familiar?

We often treat self-care as a cherry on top—something that can be done when the other to-dos have been checked off.

Catering to our most basic needs such as sleep, good food, exercise, and connection with others sets us up to be fully functioning (and kind) beings. These are non-negotiables.

Visit kimberlywilson.com/52weeks for a downloadable form to track your eating, exercise, sleep, and water-drinking habits.

Life can be so hectic that we may not realize we're missing these basics. This may lead to frustration with ourselves (Why am I so sluggish? Why can't I finish this project?) and a lack of patience with others.

I definitely find my ability to tolerate life's basic challenges (like delayed Metro trains or a pet's problematic antics) to be less than ideal when I'm not practicing self-care.

Recently I began using the app Headspace to track my meditation practices. Simple acts like sitting for 10 minutes, going for a walk, or sipping a cuppa tea can have a profound effect on bringing us to tranquility.

Are you sleeping enough, eating regularly, staying hydrated, and moving?

This week, take note of your self-care and observe how it affects your overall well-being.

Week 45: Disconnect

Look around at the faces hiding behind screens, bodies walking into traffic with eyes glued to tiny screens, and couples dining across from each other at restaurants with phones in hand.

I, too, am guilty of this constant connection at times and I'm not a fan. Yet, I find myself reaching for my beloved iPhone more often than necessary—between clients, after classes, in the elevator, and at random moments in between.

I'll bet you, too, can relate. How do we befriend our tech toys so that they *enhance* our lives rather than distract?

Some Sundays I try digital days off (an entire day offline) and notice the urge to reach for my phone out of habit. If I can resist the urge, it subsides and I'm able to go on without having to deal with what's waiting in my inbox. That's for Monday.

Another helpful shift is not reaching for my phone first thing in the morning. I charge it in another room, so it isn't by the side of the bed waiting for me when I wake up. This allows me to focus on *my* priorities before others' and start the day refueling by walking Mookie, making tea, and reviewing my *Daybook* for the day's M.I.T.

A University of Derby study found that one in eight people were addicted to their smartphones and that the average user spends 3.6 hours per day on their device. A University of Missouri study found that iPhone separation anxiety caused physical responses and diminished cognitive skills.

What are we missing by walking down sidewalks or spending time at special events staring at our screens? People are literally walking into traffic because they keep moving without being mindful of what's around them.

A friend once sent me a comic of a couple in bed on their laptops and the bubble above their heads said, "Not tonight, honey, didn't you get my email?"

I laughed sheepishly, as our means of intimate communication has taken an awkward turn.

The opportunity to connect with people far and wide through social media, email, text messaging and more is an amazing gift of our time, yet what is it doing to the connections right in front of us?

Have you ever been with a friend who keeps checking his or her phone and no, it isn't an emergency? It may feel dismissive or as if you're not engaging enough to hold their attention. Not good for the ol' self-esteem.

This week, reflect on your relationship to technology. Is it working for you? Does it feel like the right balance or is it seeping into areas of your life where it doesn't belong?

Pen snail mail. Read a physical book. Cook. Write by hand. Try a technology-free day, meal, or moment. Take control of your connection versus letting it control you.

Week 46: Bed Day

Every few months I'll toss aside my to-dos and crawl under the covers to declare Bed Day. It's my form of waving a white flag. I'm cooked, often to a delicate crisp, and need to hit the reset button surrounded by my favorite things.

Soft linens, a big bottle of water, a closed door, journal, pen, thermos of hot tea, and a pile of books is all that's needed to make this happen.

I've also been known to pull a mattress into the living room to rest fireside. It's all about the details.

The term Bed Day came up over a decade ago when I would try to take Sundays off. Surrounded by my planner and laptop, I would often stay in bed wearing whatever I'd slept in trying to sort out big-picture problems.

Over the years I've realized that this is not the way to rest (yep, slow learner) and now I choose to save strategy and brainstorming for when I'm feeling fresh and energized.

A Bed Day is an opportunity to put laundry, groceries, work, others' demands, and family obligations on hold while you rest and gain perspective. This serves as a reset button and allows you to be much more present for others and life's challenges.

Poet Audre Lorde said, "Caring for myself is not self-indulgence, it is self-preservation, and that is an act of political warfare." I declare Bed Day to be an ultimate, if not the ultimate, form of my self-care.

At times my Bed Days last only a few hours before I'm feeling refreshed with renewed energy. Others may require an entire weekend and this is common around the holidays.

The best part about Bed Days is that there are no rules. It's just you, your bed, and a deep desire to slow down.

During the 2013 Tranquility Tour, I met one woman at a Pop-Up who shared that she'd traveled hours to attend the event and even booked a hotel room for the night to have her own Bed Day without tiny-knuckled knocks on the door crying, "Mama!"

She had tears in her eyes as she shared this deep longing to escape being a 24/7 caretaker by carving out time for herself. There were numerous nods and words of encouragement throughout the room. The women understood.

This week, find space in your calendar to carve out anywhere from a few hours to an entire day or weekend (my holiday go-to) for a rejuvenating Bed Day. Gather your tools—

candles, eye pillow, tea, water, books, journal, lavender spray, comfy clothes, super-soft linens. Anything that soothes.

Begin with a luxurious soak in the tub. Add a splash of sweet almond oil and a few drops of lavender essential oil. Top with a face and/or hair mask, then saunter into your bedroom to exhale. You deserve it. And your soul will thank you.

Week 47: Gratitude

This weekend I went to an animal sanctuary to feed pumpkins to pigs. As hundreds of people tossed the round, orange fruits over the fence, the pigs came running and snorting across the fields with eyes locked on their conquest.

Their joy was contagious. I, and the many onlookers, watched them devour their treats and my heart expanded. Seeing someone engaged in what they love has a ripple effect.

Sitting around a beautifully set Thanksgiving table with loved ones is a chance to hit the pause button and slow down to reflect and express gratitude. A study from *The Wall Street Journal* claims, "Adults who frequently feel grateful have more energy, more optimism, more social connections, and more happiness than those who do not."

Recently I read a beautiful quote from Sarah Ban Breathnach's book *Simple Abundance*, "You have no idea of the countless lives you touch in the course of your lifetime."

It hit me that each interaction is an opportunity to be kind, grateful, and positive.

So rather than focusing on what's lacking, try highlighting what *is* working and develop what needs improvement over time.

Of course, we don't have to play Pollyanna, but we can strive to look at the glass as half-full by practicing regular gratitude.

Studies show that expressing gratitude can lower stress levels, improve sleep and self-esteem, enhance empathy, increase perspective, assist with overcoming trauma, and foster resilience.

This week, take time to express gratitude to someone who contributes to your well-being. Consider a colleague who helped with a project, a friend who baked a pumpkin pie, a barista who made your favorite drink, a loved one who picked you up at the airport.

Grab pen and paper and take a moment to contemplate what you're grateful for right now. A warm home, a job, a romantic relationship, a pet, a family member, a comfy bed, a dear friend, a green juice, colored pencils, health, white tea, twinkle lights— you name it!

111

Week 48: Move Mindfully

Decked out in a camel-colored velour tracksuit, I crossed the Army 10-miler finish line with a big grin and achy knees. This was November 2003 and one of my proudest moments.

I'd started running earlier that spring with a friend who coaxed me with "You can do it!" as I huffed and puffed around the monuments. After 15 minutes, I collapsed into her sedan, ready to rest.

To say athletic inclination has been a struggle for me since childhood is, well, an understatement.

In elementary school P.E. class I'd run to kick the ball—and miss. Every time. I signed up for soccer because I thought it was cheerleading and cried each time the ball came at me.

The clincher was a fourth-grade softball game where our class played the faculty while the rest of the school watched. My dear mom called me in sick while I stayed safely in the fetal position *sans* audience to observe my inability to hit a ball.

Then there was the trauma of choreographed step aerobics classes. As I fumbled on and off the step in my white high tops, I decided it was best to stick with the treadmill to avoid feeling like a class of spandex-clad ladies were silently judging me.

I'm still in recovery from that one.

When I found yoga in my early 20s, I was grateful for a way to move my body that felt intuitive. It also didn't involve an 8-count or a scary ball being thrown at me. Just a sticky mat, stretchy clothing, compassion, and my breath.

"Get moving" has been a slogan thrown our way for years. Lifestyles have become sedentary, especially when you factor in the 40+ hours each week perched in front of a screen, followed by many at home. The average American watches five hours of TV each day and is 23 pounds overweight (with over 1/3 considered obese).

Mindful movement is about finding a way to move your body while also nourishing your mind and soul. Exercise releases endorphins, and while it may be tough to put on running shoes or head to a yoga studio, it's helpful to remember how much better you feel when you do.

Find something you enjoy, or at the very least, don't dread. Did you love to dance as a child? Sign up for an adult class. Do you miss the team spirit of a group sport? Look for a local bocce, kickball, or softball league. There isn't one? Start it! Do you prefer solo adventures? Try biking, swimming, hiking, or running. Love the group experience? Check out yoga, Pilates, Barre, spinning, boxing, Zumba, or martial arts.

Studies show that those who start their day with exercise are happier and more productive. Not a morning person? Squeeze in 20 minutes whenever you can and notice the effects.

There's a way to move mindfully that will align with your energy, strength, and interest. Similar to partners, you may have to kiss a few frogs to find your prince.

This week, commit to mindful movement each day. Try a jog around the block. Stroll briskly on your morning dog walk. Ride your bike to the office. Take the stairs. Join a 5k. Try to get in 10,000 steps. Check out an assortment of drop-in classes. Do 10 jumping jacks. Go through a few sun salutations. Wander through the woods. Watch online videos and follow along. Happy mindful movement.

Week 49: Practice Yin

Come to a challenging seated yoga pose like pigeon, double pigeon, or a deep lunge with the back knee dropped. Hold for three to five minutes and breathe.

Welcome to the juicy world of yin yoga.

Yin is based in Chinese medicine and touted to have a similar effect to acupuncture—*sans* needles.

Energy flows through invisible pathways called meridians. During an acupuncture session, needles are inserted into meridians to allow blocked energy to flow.

Yin poses stimulate a certain meridian and stretch the connective tissue while a typical yoga class stretches muscle. It's a yummy, slow, quiet practice that helps counter a go, go, go pace with an infusion of nurturing and intense stretching.

Butterfly is my go-to yin pose and featured in this photo. It works wonders to stretch the lower back and stimulate the kidney meridian—considered critical to fluid energy flow. Butterfly also helps to calm the mind and ground the spirit.

Let's try it, shall we?

Bend your knees and bring the soles of your feet together to form a diamond shape. Your knees will resemble butterfly wings.

Bend forward from your hips and round your spine. Let your head rest on the soles of your feet (or a blanket, block, or pillow that you place between your head and feet). Take deep, full breaths and stay here one to five minutes. *Ommmmm.*

Since we never want pain in yoga, find that sweet spot between no sensation and too much sensation. In yoga it's referred to as "finding your edge" and a beautiful reminder for daily life.

If you feel any discomfort beyond sweet intensity, back out of the fold slightly, add a pillow under your knees, or lessen your hold time.

This week, play with butterfly pose each day and notice the effects. Also, play with finding your own sweet edge of intensity on and off the mat.

Week 50: Hollydaze

Despite the festivities, garlands, and twinkle lights, the holidays can feel a bit, well, *less* than tranquil. To combat the chaos, I've adjusted my expectations and output over the years.

No more holiday cards. No more cross-country travel. No more piles of gifts. No more trying to squeeze it all in. No more guilt. Simplicity has become my motto. The space between Christmas and New Year's Day is my rejuvenating reset button.

Our new tradition: teach yoga on Christmas eve, head to Tim's cabin in West Virginia, take in a movie and Chinese on Christmas Day, roll out the sofa bed in front of a never-ending fire, stay on said sofa bed to read, watch documentaries, and nap. Rinse and repeat for a few days.

While this may not be your cuppa tea, I encourage you to reflect on what would be your ideal holiday. Time alone. Time surrounded by family. Travel. Staying home. Big meals. Takeout. Candlelight service. Watch Santa's travel on TV. Big parties. A table for two. The ways to celebrate are endless and shift as we do.

Over the years I've dabbled with ways to keep the hollydaze feeling more tranquil inside and out. While this list is not exhaustive, the suggestions are tried and true. My hope is that they'll offer you a touch of tranquility.

1. **GET OUTSIDE.** Brisk, fresh, outdoor air helps ground me. Take in the scent of pine trees and wood smoke. Time in nature builds on a sense of interconnection. This larger view helps put things in perspective.

2. **CENTER YOURSELF.** During the hustle and bustle, it's extra important to make time for self-care. Keep up your favorite centering practices such as sipping tea, sitting on a meditation cushion, writing in your journal, practicing on your yoga mat, or soaking in the tub.

3. **GIVE.** Gift your loved ones a batch of homemade jam, a beloved book, an artisanal treat from a small business, a box of their favorite tea (or whip up your own blend), or tickets to see an exhibit. Think useful and consumable. Volunteer. Donate to a special cause. Rescue an animal. Adopt an orangutan. Sponsor a farm animal.

4. **BE KIND.** This time of year can be hard. Be gentle with yourself and others. Know we're all doing the best we can. Practice loving-kindness meditation. This may have been a hard year. Honor your growth, lessons learned, and what's to come.

5. BREATHE. When you notice your shoulders creeping up toward your ears, your heart racing while stuck in traffic, or stress building, tune into your breath. Inhale to the count of four, exhale to the count of four, repeat. Again and again.

6. TRAVEL LIGHTLY (and off-peak). Print and save the Tranquil Travel checklist at kimberlywilson.com/52weeks. Save space by rolling your clothing items into your luggage. Choose layers perfect for mixing and matching, dressing up (pearls and heels) or dressing down (clogs and denim jacket). When possible, choose off-peak travel to avoid congestion.

7. EXPRESS GRATITUDE. Take time to appreciate the little things: a warm bath, a steaming cuppa tea, a cozy bed, a devoted pet. Studies show that expressing gratitude can lower stress levels, help you sleep better, improve self-esteem, enhance empathy, and adjust your attitude.

8. GET MOVING. Exercise releases endorphins, reduces stress, and helps offset those extra holiday cookies. Put on your hiking boots or tennis shoes and hit the trails. Roll out your yoga mat and do a few sun salutations. Grab your bike and begin pedaling.

9. CELEBRATE. If you're feeling a bit of the bah humbug blues, put on your favorite holiday film, create a playlist of festive tunes, go see a childhood treat such as *The Nutcracker*, and put up a few holiday decorations to evoke good memories. Review the year and list highlights.

10. DREAM. Create time to daydream about the new year. What do you hope to see, taste, touch, smell, and hear in the coming year? List everything that comes to mind and focus on the experiences you hope to have.

Wishing you a holiday filled with your favorite things. Make this season meaningful.

Week 51: Be Kind

I was in New York City hauling my overstuffed luggage up and down the subway stairs. After a week-long workshop, I headed to Central Park for a little sunshine before boarding the bus back to D.C. Unfortunately, that meant multiple staircases with a heavy load in sweltering August heat.

The two times I needed assistance crawling up the stairs, a kind soul would grab the other end of the bag and help me to the street. I didn't ask. Someone paused, noticed my struggle, and offered a hand.

It was two summers ago and I still remember that gesture with gratitude. Kindness. Although kindness seems like a basic concept, I looked up the definition to see its official description: benevolence, a desire to do good to others, considerate, or helpful.

Every day we are granted numerous opportunities to be kind or not so kind. There are many ways to offer a gesture of kindness: wash your colleagues' dishes in the office kitchen, hold the door open, give a compliment, offer kudos, let someone into your lane, donate to a special cause, plant a community garden, listen fully to your partner, recycle, smile, say "please" and "thank you," wish your building security guard a good day, think before you speak, practice metta meditation, bake cookies for your office.

While it's easy to be kind when you're responding to another's kindness, what about the meanies? I hear ya, it's not easy. Plato said, "Be kind, for everyone you meet is fighting a hard battle." I try to keep this in mind when I come across Debbie Downer or an equally challenging character.

We don't know what that person is going through at the moment, so rather than taking a rude comment or tone personally, try responding with kindness. It's not easy, but it may lessen your guilt for reacting, and ideally is a ray of sunshine in their day.

An act of kindness has a ripple effect on our mood. When I respond to the lady at the post office with a smile versus a snippy reaction to her not-so-friendly disposition, I leave feeling better. When I engage with a nasty tone, I get worked up, feel guilty for not being my best self, and leave feeling as if my tail is tucked between my legs.

Then I remember this quote by the Dalai Lama, "Be kind whenever possible. It is always possible." Yes, even with the unfriendly receptionist, condescending boss, disengaged partner, or customer service rep just trying to do her job.

This week, practice being kind in a variety of situations. Challenge yourself in those times that normally set you off—traffic, waiting for your child or partner to get ready, dealing with an unreasonable complaint, poor service at a restaurant. May kindness prevail.

Week 52: Reflect

The end of the year. Another completed chapter. Let's tie a ceremonial bow around it and honor your evolution—highlights, lessons learned, struggles, dreams, experiences. Each of these played a role in your year's unfurling.

To jolt memories, set aside time to flip through places you kept notes and dates, such as your *Daybook*, planner, online calendar, and journal. Scroll through your photos for visual cues. Pull out cards, ticket stubs, conference swag, and/or exhibit brochures (I keep these items in a shoe box wrapped in pretty paper labeled "memories"). Collect any mementos you may have tucked away from this year and pile it on your kitchen table.

According to Sarah Susanka, author of *The Not So Big Life: Making Room for What Really Matters* (*Tranquility du Jour* podcast #181), "The end-of-year review process is very similar to sowing seeds. When you plant a garden, you don't sit and stare at the seeds until they sprout. You know that some will germinate and some will not, but it is not up to you to make them grow. All you can do is set the conditions for their growth with good soil, adequate water, and the right amount of sun. And that's what this exercise does—and while you are sowing seeds during this period, you can be enjoying the fruits of the previous year's harvest at the same time."

Here are a few questions to help you start the process:

- How did you spend your time? There are 168 hours/week and 8,760 hours/year. Where did yours go? Break it down into categories such as family, creativity, work, spirituality, etc. Compare where it went to where you'd like to see it go next year.
- What journeys did you take?
- What were your accomplishments and disappointments?
- What lessons did you learn?
- How have you grown from this time last year?
- How do you hope to show up this time next year?

Grab writing tools and paper. Take a sip of something yummy and start listing what you recall from the year in no particular order and answer the above questions. Capture big moments

(e.g. started graduate school) along with tiny ones (e.g. sipped a cherry limeade at the drive-in with mom). Let the list flow.

Design a visual representation of the year by printing an assortment of photos and creating a collage. Or if you're more techie, use an app like Collage Creator to assemble an electronic history that can be a desktop or image to share with loved ones.

I paste a beautiful image into my art journal and list memories on it with a Sharpie. This reminds me of the year's ups and down, allows me to express gratitude for what transpired, and honor the evolution.

After this process (which can take days, by the way), review your answers, images, hopes, and dreams. Light a candle to honor losses. Acknowledge how every experience has made your year unique. Set an intention for what you hope to see unfold next year. Allow this process to nurture who you are and who you are becoming. *Sans* judgment, simply observation filled with loving-kindness.

Bonus 1: Beauty Routine

We recently had our bathroom painted bubble gum pink, so I had to remove all products from the shelves. I was horrified. Eight face oils, two face sprays, two big bottles of sweet almond oil, ten perfumes, ten red lipsticks, three eye creams, four face moisturizers, two mascaras, three eyeliners, face powder, toothpaste, all-natural and regular deodorant, hairspray, floss, razor, face scrub, leave-in conditioner, shampoo, soap, and three hair shine sprays. These filled an entire medium-sized wicker basket.

When putting each item back on the shelf, I dusted it off and asked myself whether it was necessary. Many products were gifts or purchased from a small-batch artisan, while some were simply unnecessary, expired, and taking up space. Those were tossed or donated.

Since then I've paid particular attention to what I reach for on a daily or weekly basis and it's quite simple.

FACE: cleanser, face oils, mascara, lipstick

BODY: sweet almond oil, deodorant, perfume, soap, razor

TEETH: toothpaste, floss, electric toothbrush

HAIR: shampoo/conditioner, leave-in conditioner, hair shine/serum spray

The rest of the items were simply fluff (e.g. the citrus face spray), duplicates (e.g. red lipstick from Paris), or options (e.g. different types/brands of face oil).

Take a closer look at what you're using regularly and pare down to the basics. One face oil is probably enough. Okay, two if you want a blend in addition to plain argan oil. One or two lipsticks work. One signature scent perfume is sufficient.

Pretend your bathroom is getting painted and place all your toiletries into a basket. Pull out what you need over a few weeks and donate or recycle what's left. If you have a few items in the basket that were gifts or are too hard to part with, add them to your beauty routine and use them up.

Pare your beauty routine down to the essentials this week. This process will help with travel, simplify your morning routine, and get rid of clutter.

Bonus 2: De-stress

Mindfulness has become a buzzword showing up on covers of magazines, at yoga retreats, and at psychotherapy conferences. When I was exposed to it years ago, I saw it as the silver bullet—a technique to help quiet a busy mind, regulate the emotions, and change the shape of the brain!

In the late 70s, when Jon Kabat-Zinn created Mindfulness-Based Stress Reduction (MBSR), he focused on patients whom the medical system was unable to heal and introduced them to mindfulness meditation, body scan, and mindful yoga through an eight-week program. The program requires daily 45-minute practices outside of the 2.5-hour weekly meetings. Pre-and post-tests are conducted and have found that these practices lowered patients' pain, stress, anxiety, and depression.

Mindfulness is defined as moment-to-moment, non-judgmental awareness and studies have shown measurable physical changes in the brains of people who routinely meditate. The outer layer of the brain that contains our thinking, reasoning, and decision-making is thicker in practitioners who meditate 45 minutes every day. The insula is also thicker and is involved in coordinating the brain, body, emotions, and thoughts to help us make better decisions.

I want to introduce a few techniques that I've found particularly helpful on my mindfulness journey and I hope that they will help you find grace in the midst of daily stress.

STOP. This acronym is a good reminder when you are triggered by events such as a late train or an insensitive email. S stands for stop. T stands for take a breath. O stands for observe what's happening. P stands for proceed with awareness. Viktor Frankl, author of Man's Search for Meaning, says, "Between stimulus and response there is a space. In that space is our power to choose our response. In our response lies our growth and our freedom." Practicing STOP provides space between a stimulus and response.

COME TO YOUR SENSES. Shift your focus from a busy mind by tapping into your five senses—hearing, sight, touch, smell, or taste. Notice the sounds around you. Be an observer of what you see. Observe the feeling of your clothes on your skin or the chair under your hips. Tune in to any scents. Sip your tea or eat your scone with full attention.

EXAMINE YOUR THOUGHTS. With 50,000-70,000 thoughts a day, it's no wonder we feel frazzled. Throughout the day, notice what's on your mind. Are you thinking about something that happened earlier? Are you planning for a future event? Are you worrying about what may happen? Are you engaged in negative self-talk? Are you daydreaming? No judgment, just observe. In yoga, we refer to the busy mind as "monkey mind." Think of a darling orangutan swinging through the forest limb to limb, tree to tree. That's the nature of our minds. By intentionally noticing where the mind has traveled, we can better understand ourselves and exercise our mindfulness muscle by returning to the present moment. A 2010 study found that people's minds wander 46.9 percent of the time, and during these times the participants were feeling unhappy.

Practice these three techniques and notice how your stress levels and overall happiness shift. Our thoughts are not reality, but more part of our interior landscape. As we become more aware of the inner workings of our mind, we can find that juicy freedom between stimulus and response.

Bonus 3: Capsule Wardrobe

I opened my closet and saw an overflowing sea of black with a few token colored vintage pieces sprinkled in. There were numerous fancy skirts and sparkly items that didn't align with my therapist or yoga teacher wardrobe. It was time to do some culling.

I kept hearing about a capsule wardrobe—a collection of a few essential items of clothing that don't go out of fashion and can easily be mixed and matched. This seemed like the optimal way to make sure I always had something to wear without having to overplan or keep buying new things.

Stopping into discount stores, vintage boutiques, or resale shops used to be a favorite pastime. I'd come away with something new at a great price, but rarely found myself wearing it. Instead I returned to my staples again and again. I have duplicates of a few staples, so that I don't even have to wait for it to come out of the laundry.

I cut out the retail browsing, went through my closet piece by piece, and pared down to the basics (plus a few tutus and sequined items). A capsule wardrobe doesn't just help with day-to-day dressing; it's also a huge relief when you're packing to travel.

Begin by observing your shopping habits and notice if regular retail therapy is helping (if you're a stylist) or hindering (if you're not). Swap lunchtime browsing with book reading in a café. Try brunch with friends instead of weekend shopping.

Next, closet time and it's best to set aside a few hours for this. Pull everything out of your closets, drawers, or boxes and set the pieces onto your bed. Inspect each item carefully considering how often you wear it, if you still like it, and if you feel good in it. Create love, let go, and maybe piles. Donate the let go. Contemplate the maybe.

Maybe you love your structured clothing, but now work from home. Or you're down on the floor playing with children a lot of your day. Keep clothing that matches your lifestyle. If you're in transition, hold onto the clothes that you plan to return to. If not, let those maybes go.

Go through the love pile for capsule wardrobe possibilities. Pull out your go-tos such as black pants, crisp white shirt, blazer, or shift dress. Keep narrowing your favorites down to those that can be dressed up or down, will mix and match, and fit your lifestyle. Sticking with neutral colors such as navy, black, or beige helps.

You may choose a 10-piece capsule or a 50-piece capsule. The number doesn't matter as much as the intention to keep only items you love, wear what feels good, save time by sticking with the basics, and save money by curbing the mindless shopping.

This week, create or curate your capsule wardrobe.

Bonus 4: Hydrate

It's mid-day, I'm on the Metro heading to a meeting across the river (aka Virginia) and begin to feel parched. I reach inside my vegan tote, feeling around for my pink water bottle. I've left it back at the office. Panic sets in.

If I don't have my water bottle with me at all times, I begin to get anxious. It's even bedside when I'm sleeping, on the edge of the tub during my soaks, and next to my yoga mat when I'm practicing.

Feeling flushed or having heart palpitations when without a water bottle may sound extreme, yet a full water bottle has become a security blanket over the years. No, I've never been stranded in a desert, so I'm not sure where this fear comes from, but let's just take it at face value. Hydration is essential to my health and yours (she says as she takes a big sip from her full pink water bottle).

Adult bodies are made up of 60% water (brain and heart 73%, lungs 83%, skin 64%, muscles and kidneys 79%, and bones 31%), according to the Journal of Biological Chemistry.

Cells, tissues, and organs in our body need water to survive. Water helps form saliva, flushes body waste, lubricates joints, delivers oxygen, aids in digestion, cushions and protects vital organs, and regulates our internal body temperature through sweating and respiration.

Ideally, we should consume six to eight 8-ounce glasses of water daily. You'll know you're staying hydrated if your urine is colorless or pale.

You can even boost brainpower by drinking water. One study in Frontiers in Human Neuroscience found that participants who drank water before performing cognitive tasks reacted faster than those who didn't.

Drinking water may help you lose weight. Some times when we're feeling hungry, actually we're thirsty. Try drinking a glass of water before reaching for that mid-day snack because that may be all you need.

Struggling with headaches? When the body is low on water, blood vessels dilate and then swell which may cause or worsen headaches.

If plain tap water isn't your thing, add a cucumber, orange, lemon, or lime slice to it. I've been adding packets of crystallized lemon or grapefruit to my water and love the tart effect.

Be creative and get your daily dose of H20 through tasty fruits and veggies. Watermelon, strawberries, grapefruit, cantaloupe, and peaches have the highest water content (88-92% water) in the fruit family. Cucumber, lettuce, zucchini, radish, celery, tomato, and cabbage have the highest content (93-96% water) in the veggie family.

Track your water intake this week and note your feeling of overall well-being. Do you notice feeling sluggish when you have less than is recommended? How does it feel when you get a full 64 ounces in your belly throughout the day? If you don't already have a water bottle, pick one up and tote it everywhere.

Confession, I even take mine to restaurants as I don't want to have to wait for my first glass or refills—I'm sure to stay hydrated without relying on the full attention of the server. Happy hydrating!

Bonus 5: Accessorize

Decked in layers of sparkly necklaces, a sequin beanie, glittery ring, sparkly earrings, a mesh tutu, and silver sequin shoes, I realized I may have on that one (or three) thing(s) too many for the holiday fête. However, I couldn't bear to surrender one of the items, so off I went over-accessorized.

Accessorizing transforms a basic white tee and black legging ensemble into a work of art. Add ballet flats, pearls, and a crisp white shirt over the tee for an ode to Audrey. Try pointed black heels, a black blazer, and headscarf for sass. Consider a knit wrap, tall boots, infinity cowl, and beanie for cozy.

The options are endless and you probably have many outfit-transforming accessories at your fingertips.

Two important accessories to don daily are a smile and positive attitude. These are magnetic and project confidence. In addition to warm smiles, infuse your wardrobe with a few varied and key accessories.

Accessorizing is a skill that can be honed and perfected with practice. There's no need to be "matchy" with coordinated shoes, handbags, and extras. If you've walked the streets of New York, Paris, or San Francisco, you've seen unrelated pieces pulled together with flair. Somehow, it works.

To start, select your favorite accessories to build on. These will become traits of your signature style. Is it big sunnies? Chunky layered necklaces. Tall boots year round. Vintage buttons or brooches on jackets. Dangly rhinestone earrings. Tattoos. Big belts. Sparkly cocktail rings. Colorful neck or head scarves.

The right accessories embellish your basics and the options are endless.

ARMS: Arm warmers. Wood or metal bangles. Rings.

LEGS: Leg warmers. Over-the-knee socks.

FEET: Flats. Boots. Heels. Flip-flops (a must for pedis). Sneakers. Clogs.

HEAD: Headbands. Scarves to tie in your hair, wrap around your neck, or around your head à la Audrey. Tie a thin scarf around your wrist. Eyeglasses. Sunnies. Hats. Barrettes.

EARS: Earrings make your face sparkle.

NECK: Long beads, chains, and chokers—use in layers to add the perfect accent.

BODY: Outerwear such as a trench, vintage bomber, denim, and faux fur (straight from Grandma's closet). Bags such as a patent clutch, luggage, overnighter, and an everyday. Belts. Flower pins. Brooches. Tattoos.

Browse vintage or secondhand shops. Go through your mum's jewelry box and ask for family heirlooms. Peruse Etsy.com for handmade treasures created by female artists or make your own. Try DIY ideas splashed all over Pinterest. Turn your simple staples into a playful artistic display.

This week, play with the accessories you have on hand. Add a hand-knitted cowl to your outfit for a pop of color. Try a brooch on your faux fur coat. Add a sparkly headband or earrings to your day ensemble. Layer an assortment of necklaces typically worn solo.

Let your inner artist out to play and enjoy how accessories add flair to your every day wear.

Savvy Sources

MINDFULNESS

Wherever You Go, There You Are: Mindfulness Meditation in Everyday Life by Jon Kabat-Zinn

10% Happier: How I Tamed the Voice in My Head, Reduces Stress Without Losing My Edge, and Found Self-Help That Actually Works—A True Story by Dan Harris

Peace Is Every Step: The Path of Mindfulness in Everyday Life by Thich Nhat Hanh

Tranquility du Jour podcasts #171, #267, 317, #341, #356, #357

STYLE AND BEAUTY

Lessons from Madame Chic: 20 Stylish Secrets I Learned While Living in Paris by Jennifer Scott

Forever Chic: Frenchwomen's Secrets for Timeless Beauty, Style, and Substance by Tish Jett

Ooh La La!: French Women's Secrets to Feeling Beautiful Every Day by Jamie Cat Callan

Tranquility du Jour podcasts #179, #221, #232, #289, #310, #338, #351

CREATIVITY

The Accidental Creative: How to Be Brilliant at a Moment's Notice by Todd Henry

Big Magic: Creative Living Beyond Fear by Elizabeth Gilbert

Art Before Breakfast: A Zillion Ways to be More Creative No Matter How Busy You Are by Danny Gregory

Tranquility du Jour podcasts #78, #122, #152, #154, #184, #231, #238, #273

YOGA

Jivamukti Yoga: Practices for Liberating Body and Soul by Sharon Gannon and David Life

Bringing Yoga to Life: The Everyday Practice of Enlightened Living by Donna Farhi

Yoga for Emotional Balance: Simple Practices to Help Relieve Anxiety and Depression by Bo Forbes

Tranquility du Jour podcasts #29, #126, #194, #219, #246, #305, #307, #315, #355

WRITING

On Writing Well: The Classic Guide to Writing Nonfiction by William Zinsser

The True Secret of Writing: Connecting Life with Language by Natalie Goldberg

The Forest for the Trees: An Editor's Advice to Writers by Betsy Lerner

Tranquility du Jour podcasts #33, #96, #311, #337, #353

PRODUCTIVITY

Manage Your Day-To-Day: Build Your Routine, Find Your Focus, and Sharpen Your Creative Mind by Jocelyn Glei

Essentialism: The Disciplined Pursuit of Less by Greg McKeown

The Power of Habit: Why We Do What We Do In Life and Business by Charles Duhigg

Tranquility du Jour podcasts #199, #226, #306, #343, 352

MINIMALISM

You Can Buy Happiness (and It's Cheap): How One Woman Radically Simplified Her Life and How You Can Too by Tammy Strobel

The Big Tiny: A Built-It-Myself Memoir by Dee Williams

Choosing the Simply Luxurious Life: A Modern Woman's Guide by Shannon Ables

Tranquility du Jour podcasts #181, #207, #210, #253, #259, #340

VEGETARIANISM

The Good Karma Diet: Eat Gently, Feel Amazing, Age in Slow Motion by Victoria Moran

Why We Love Dogs, Eat Pigs, and Wear Cows: An Introduction to Carnism by Melanie Joy

Living the Farm Sanctuary Life: The Ultimate Guide to Eating Mindfully, Living Longer, and Feeling Better Every Day by Gene Baur

Tranquility du Jour podcasts #227, #236, #240, #258, #316, #354

Farewell

Congratulations! You have journeyed through another year.

We're given 52 weeks to work toward our dreams and each year holds the promise of possibility. The tools within this *Journal* are a sampling of the ways I strive to infuse my days with tranquility. My wish is that they help your days feel abundant and meaningful.

While no day is perfect, strive to do one thing every day that scares you (per Eleanor Roosevelt), believe that remaining tight in a bud is more painful than blooming (per Anais Nin), remember that a small group of thoughtful, committed citizens can change the world (per Margaret Mead), keep the creative channel open knowing that your expression is unique and if you block it, it will be lost and the world will not have it (per Martha Graham), and remind yourself that everyone is fighting a hard battle (per Plato).

Return to this *Journal* again and again. Use it for inspiration when you need a pick-me-up. Reread the essays when seeking new ways of showing up in the world. Review what you've written or highlighted for gentle reminders of what matters most to you. Let it become a trusted friend.

You are a beautiful soul with a special gift. There is no one else like you. As Zen teacher Shunryu Suzuki reminds us, "You're perfect just as you are and you could use a little improvement." Remember your divine perfection. Move toward your ideal self. Honor your growth. And let yourself play.

Yours on the journey,
Kimberly Wilson

About Kimberly Wilson

I'm a writer, therapist, designer of the TranquiliT clothing line, and founder of Tranquil Space—named among the top 25 yoga studios in the world. I dream of Paris and global animal welfare.

You'll often find me sipping fragrant tea, practicing yoga on a leopard-print mat, or leading retreats around the world. My work has been featured in *US News & World Reports*, *Washingtonian*, *Fast Company*, and *Yoga Journal*.

I live in the petite Pink Palace in Washington, D.C. with a rescue kitty, a rescue pug, and a non-rescued beau. Indulge in "tranquilosophy" via my blog and podcast, *Tranquility du Jour*.

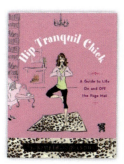 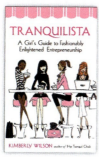    

 @kimberlywilson 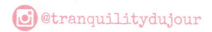 @tranquilitydujour  @tranquilitydujour

kimberlywilson.com

Made in the USA
Charleston, SC
08 March 2016